Spin Roulette Gold

Secrets of Beating the Wheel

Frank Scoblete

Bonus Books, Inc., Chicago

01   00   99   98   97   5   4   3   2   1

Library of Congress Cataloging-in-Publication Data

Scoblete, Frank.
   Spin roulette gold : secrets of beating the wheel / Frank
Scoblete.
     p.   cm.
   Includes bibliographical references and index.
   ISBN 1-56625-074-9 (alk. paper)
   1. Roulette. 2. Gambling systems. I. Title.
GV1309.S36   1997
795.2'3—dc21   97-11215

Bonus Books, Inc.
160 East Illinois Street
Chicago, Illinois 60611

Printed in the United States of America

*This book is dedicated to three teachers who taught at
Our Lady Of Angels elementary school in
Bay Ridge, Brooklyn, in the late 1950s, early 1960s*

three wonderful people who had a profound effect on my life:

*to Sister Patricia Michael,
who wouldn't let me get away with anything,*

*to Brother Jonathan,
who told me I had writing talent,*

and

*to Brother Barnabas,
who gave me the ball and the confidence to take the clutch shots*

whether you are here or in the hereafter

Thank You.

Good breeding consists in concealing how much
we think of ourselves and how little we think
of the other person.

—Mark Twain

Contents

Acknowledgments
and Foreword

Prose is easy. Numbers are hard. And roulette is essentially a game of numbers, numbers and more numbers. My initial design for this book was simply to lay out the various strategies and let the reader go to the wheels and record all those spins and see how the strategies held up. This attitude had more to do with my enjoyment of the act of writing than my dislike in recording things. I do like to interview people; talk to people; recount my experiences. I don't particularly like standing at a roulette wheel recording numbers. So I wasn't going to do it.

Thankfully, my wife, the beautiful A.P., convinced me that roulette players love the numbers, want to see the numbers, and will use the numbers to help them structure their attack on the game. "Given the choice of a book with just numbers and a book with just your writing," she said, "the true roulette player would buy the numbers." So much for prose.

This book therefore has the numbers — over 10,000 recorded spins of actual roulette wheels — 3,800 from a single wheel — to go with what I consider the best possible strategies to overcome a game with a (usually) frighteningly high house edge. Remember, the numbers recorded throughout this book are from real wheels, not computer simulations. And real people had to record these numbers: Gary, Heidi, Wayne, Howard T. Mann and Alene Paone. I even recorded 500 numbers myself.

Throughout the book, I have used **bold** lettering for the black numbers, regular lettering for the red numbers, and *italics* for the *0* and *00*.

I hope that after reading this book you will be able to spin roulette gold!

1

The Lure and Lore of Roulette

It's no secret that roulette was and still is the game of choice in Europe. It's also no secret that many a noble fortune has been won and, sadly, still many more fortunes have been ignobly lost on this spinning wheel of Dame Fortune. For the European, roulette is almost a mystical game where countless betting systems — often arcane, sometimes incomprehensible, always futile — have been devised to harness luck and overcome the house edge. Those of us who read history are well aware of all the tales concerning the damage roulette did to the aristocratic societies of England and France in the 18th and 19th centuries. Roulette is still played with a passion on the continent.

We are also aware of those delicious few tales of gamblers "breaking the bank" at Monte Carlo or taking off some other casino for fabulous wealth. Many of these tales are true, although often greatly exaggerated. This last is no shock as hyperbole and gambling go hand in hand. In fishing, a fisherman will talk about the one that *got away*. "It was THIS big!" In gambling we talk about the one we *caught*. We take "this big" and make it "THIS BIG!" — to make the story more entertaining, more lively, more dramatic, and to make us, of course, more heroic. People love stories of winners, preferably big winners, and tellers of gambling tales know this and, well, they embellish a bit on their tales. Oh, yes, the bank at Monte Carlo was broken . . . but it was only the bank of *one table* and it was actually broken a dozen times in relatively quick succession. I guess in today's parlance, it would be the contents of one chip tray that were hauled away. Now, that's a lot of money to be sure but it isn't going to close a casino down to lose the bank of a table, even several times. Yet it does sound nice to say — "I broke the bank!" As *Spin Roulette Gold* is a no-nonsense look at playing and, hopefully, winning at roulette, it will not be packed with delightful stories of winners and their adventures throughout history. Besides, Russell T. Barnhart's wonderful book, *Beat the Wheel* (Carol Publishing), is filled with stories of people who have won THIS MUCH and I recommend that you read this excellent work.

The origins of roulette are somewhat shrouded and probably go back to prehistoric times, as does much of gambling. We do know, for instance, that the ancient Romans used the spinning of chariot wheels as part of their games and that the ancient Greeks would spin shields to divine Fortune's will. Many primitive societies used revolving sticks or pointers as part of their games and, more importantly, as part of their religions. Often the ancient peoples spun their wheels or sticks to ascertain the will of their gods. "If the wheel lands on *this,* I will take an ox and let it loose in the field to honor the great god Umba. If it lands on *that,* I will sacrifice the ox to his wife, Amba." And just as often they spun those wheels and sticks in pursuit of lucre: "I will spin that wheel and if it lands on this, I win your ox! If it lands on that, you win my wife!" Don't laugh. This last, the betting of one's wife in a final, desperate attempt to win back one's lost fortune, is a story told in many a cautionary tale from ancient India to 19th-century England. The joke "take my wife, please" is no joke in some circles.

The first recognizable roulette wheels appeared in the 17th century. The game was called *hoca* and it was a favorite of the French statesman Cardinal Mazarin who used it to increase the treasury of the young Louis XIV. Mazarin opened many a casino in France and the money rolled in for both him and Louis XIV. Of course, when Mazarin died, *hoca* was outlawed and anyone found playing it was executed. Other primitive versions of roulette existed during this time period as well.

History tells us that the game of roulette as we now know it was firmly established by the end of the 18th century in Europe and elsewhere. Indeed, the Swiss economy of the late 18th century was helped immeasurably by the manufacturing of roulette wheels for the courts and gaming rooms of Russia, France, Germany, Turkey, India and England. The Swiss manufactured wheels of unparalleled elegance and precision. Their wheels were — for that time period — marvels of precision, beautifully balanced, crafted with grace and style and, as such, they were in great demand. Interestingly enough, while the Swiss lovingly made the wheels, they scorned the game. Roulette was not played in Switzerland.

By the end of the 19th century, the casino at Monte Carlo was in full swing, and what started as a two-wheel roulette operation in a dusty barn had become a glittering casino showplace for the rich and famous. People travelled from all over the world to play the tables at Monte Carlo and then return home, less wealthy, still unwise but brimming with stories of their adventures in the ultimate temple of chance. Monte Carlo is still a magic name in gaming circles and few casino gamblers' lives are complete without a visit to its famed betting parlors.

Millions of people love to play the game of roulette; they play it with passion and daring. But you don't have to be European to love the game. Despite the fact that the game is considered the "third" table game in America (behind blackjack and craps), roulette's popularity seems to be growing among American players. The total number of roulette tables and roulette players in America today dwarfs by comparison the total number of tables at any time in history. In the major casinos of Las Vegas, Reno, Lake Tahoe, the Midwest, Mississippi and Atlantic City, you will encounter hundreds of roulette tables being played with equal fervor and intensity to the roulette tables of Europe (despite the fact that roulette on the

standard American double-zero wheel offers a much worse
game than does the European single-zero wheel).

When I first started playing seriously in the casinos, I was
only dimly aware of the roulette subculture; a subculture
every bit as enthusiastic and real as the blackjack subculture,
although somewhat less cantankerous and argumentative,
and decidedly less prolific. What makes roulette such an ob-
session among its devotees? I believe that there are four minor
reasons and one major reason.

Minor Reasons

One: tradition.
Roulette has a history that is known and respected by
many of its devoted players. There's a little bit of that Monte
Carlo magic at every roulette wheel even if it's in the meanest
sawdust joint. Dice players often have no idea that they are
playing a game with a history — indeed, a history that goes
far back to the earliest humans who carved out symbols on
bones and then "rolled them bones" to discover what fate had
in store. Often roulette aficionados ensconce themselves in its
past, in its splendor, and can tell you the names of all the great
roulette players of history and recite all the stories of the big
scores and bigger falls. Even if you're betting the table minimum, there often appears to be a fortune riding on every spin
since so many different colored chips (often with no indication
of their value) are piled on the layout.

Two: elegance.
Roulette is a leisurely, often elegant game. Players are
rarely rushed to place bets and dealers rarely seem to rush in
paying off those bets. There is a general sense of civility and
decorum. The game is associated with James Bond and aris-
tocracy and casual money and evening dress.

Three: systems.
Roulette offers the players a host of betting options, all of
which contribute to the creation of elaborate systems of play
that often result in short-term success. Most gaming systems
that we know of today were first created with roulette in

mind. There are a number of sophisticated-sounding systems that roulette players enjoy employing: the Martingale, the Grand Martingale and the d'Alembert to name a few. The names all sound so wonderful.

Four: opportunity.

Roulette has some of the highest paybacks found at a table game. To be sure, the player faces stiff odds and a high house edge, but the lure of big money returns is a compelling motivation to play. Also, roulette appeals to many different temperaments. If you want a lot of little wins, you can bet the "even-money" bets where you'll win approximately half the time. Certain betting schemes allow you to win small sums almost *every time* (and get clobbered on occasion). Some gamblers like this. Still other gamblers enjoy the thrill that comes with hitting a longshot for relatively big money. Roulette affords this player his big score. So opportunity seems to knock at roulette.

Major Reason

Anticipation.

Like the Carly Simon song says: "Anticipation is making me wait!" and that, I believe, is the key element in roulette's success these past centuries. Waiting. Because of the leisurely nature of roulette, the players get to build up their anticipatory sets waiting for the spinning of the ball, the dropping of the ball, the bouncing of the ball, and the eventual landing of the ball in the pocket. Over the years I have become convinced that part of the thrill of gambling has as much to do with the anticipation of the decision as it does with the actuality of the decision itself. I think many gamblers become hooked on their own adrenaline because of this. I believe that the "gambler's high" that people refer to is an actual, psychological-physical state — much like the runner's high — and that a significant part of that psychological-physical state is created by the sense of excitement as one waits for the game to begin. In roulette, you get plenty of time between decisions to overcome the feelings you had after the last decision (happiness at a win, misery for a loss) and build yourself up for the next decision. Roulette is an adrenaline-friendly game for that reason. For roulette players, this adrenaline rush can even be used as a playing strategy — as I shall show in this book — that can decrease overall risk and increase one's overall pleasure.

Can Roulette Be Beaten?

Despite the fact that a multitude of systems exist for attacking roulette, most of them cannot overcome the house edge because they are layout strategies which are essentially betting or money-management strategies. As such, they cannot overcome the casino edges that range from 1.35 percent to 7.89 percent, depending on the wheel and the type of bet placed. All you're doing when you employ a layout strategy is putting your money down on a given proposition or set of propositions, and hoping for a good dose of luck, while accepting the fact that the casino will take a slice of your win as its vig (vig is casinoese for the tax the casino takes on your winning wager). As you will note when you look at the diagrams of the wheels coming up, the layout of the numbers for betting purposes has little to do with the placement of the numbers on the wheel itself — regardless of whether we're viewing the single-zero European wheel or the double-zero American wheel. The placement of the numbers was done purposely to prevent the second kind of strategy, *wheel strategies,* from being employed by gamblers.

Wheel strategies have a chance at success because they take advantage of imperfections in the mechanism itself. The argument goes that no roulette mechanism is perfect and that some are considerably less perfect than others. On the latter, a player might be able to find a certain number, or certain numbers, or sections of numbers on the wheel where the hits are way out of proportion to what probability theory suggests — enough so that the house edge is significantly overcome. Thus, the game is turned in favor of the player. However, to play accurate wheel strategies does require quite a bit of time and effort. You have to track the wheel; that is, record several thousand hits of a given mechanism to ascertain with a high degree of certainty that the wheel is indeed biased. For some roulette players, the amount of time and the great effort that go into clocking wheels are in and of themselves pleasurable; for others, tackling accurate wheel strategies is a chore and a bore. You'll have to decide which group you belong to.

The third type of strategy is also referred to as wheel clocking or wheel tracking but it has nothing to do with long-range tracking of hits to see if a wheel is biased. Instead, in this type of wheel tracking, a player attempts to determine what sector of numbers the ball will most probably land in after it makes its descent. The player does this by judging the ball's speed in relation to the rotation of the wheel. The way a baseball player determines where a fly ball will ultimately land and runs to the spot to be there waiting for it, or a scientist determines where a satellite will reenter earth's atmosphere, is the same way the wheel clocker decides where the ball will lose steam and drop — all this in relation to the numbers charging toward it on the wheel. Generally, there is a 15- to 20-second window of betting opportunity for players who can perform this feat, as it is generally the last few revolutions that give the visual wheel tracker the necessary information.

There is a fourth, though quite controversial, strategy that involves neither playing a biased wheel nor playing a betting strategy on the layout, nor visually tracking the ball in its orbit. It is called "Signature Sighting" and involves *playing the dealer.* In this style of play, one observes the dealer to see if accurate predictions can be made *vis-à-vis* the dealer's spinning of the ball. Some dealers, the argument goes, have developed a rather mechanical approach to the game and tend to spin the ball the same way each time. Since a dealer always picks the ball from the last number that hit and then spins it a breath or two later, some dealers will tend to have predictable "spacing" between their hits. We might be capable of reading these dealers, so this theory goes, just as we are capable of reading a biased wheel.

Why Play Roulette?

For the serious player, the player interested in profit first and fun second (if at all), roulette can offer an opportunity to make some decent money at the gaming tables — if the player is willing to put in the necessary time to develop one of the strategies that can overcome the house's edge. That is a big *if.* For you, this book will contain all you need to know to tackle what is called "advantage play." I'll look at clocking strategies and how to determine with a high degree of certainty that you are, indeed, playing biased wheels.

For the recreational player, the player interested in fun first, profit second, there are many interesting ways to approach the game — some of which might offer a chance for substantial gain without having to put the time and effort into clocking wheels. I'll offer short-term strategies that might, just might, be able to turn the game around for you, or at least give you a chance to take advantage of potentially biased wheels or possible dealer signatures. Of course, not every roulette player is interested in advantage play, real or potential. Many just like to play the game and are quite content to employ a host of layout or betting strategies, knowing in the end that all such strategies must succumb to the house edge. Some excellent layout strategies are in this book as well.

You have to determine what kind of roulette player you want to be. My personal advice for recreational players is to take one of the strategies based on *potentially* biased wheels, dealer signatures, or the like and employ them in the short run. These will only take a little effort but might offer great rewards. For those of you who aren't interested in even this kind of effort, I have layout strategies that require no real effort to employ, just some discipline. Any layout strategies that I discuss are handled in such a way as to give two results: one, decreasing one's overall risk by reducing one's total exposure to the house's edge over time; and, two, increasing one's adrenaline rush that comes with anticipation. In short, I want to maximize pleasure and diminish overall risk in my layout strategies. In that I am following in the footsteps of the great Greek philosopher, Epicurus, who believed that the only truth in life was to maximize pleasure and minimize pain. I'll buy that.

2

The Procedures and Wagers of Roulette

There are two roulette games: the American and the European. The roulette playing area for both is divided into two parts. On one end is a large wheel (approximately three feet in diameter) that is divided into three distinct layers: the backtrack, which is the stationary outer frame that has the groove where the ball is spun; the bottom track, which is where the ball falls when it leaves the backtrack; and the wheel head, which is the spinning wheel that contains the slots or pockets for the ball to fall into. Roulette balls actually come in a variety of sizes between that of a marble and a ping-pong ball and each roulette table usually has two balls assigned it, one large and one small. It is of interest to note that on the bottom track there are a number of bumpers or barriers that prevent the ball from making a clean dive into the numbered pockets. When the ball hits these barriers, it tends to jump. This is a protection to make sure that the game is random and that it is virtually impossible to predict in advance where the ball will drop. The second part of the roulette playing area is the layout where the bets are placed, the details of which I shall discuss shortly.

When a player comes to the roulette table, he places his money down on the layout and asks for chips. While the player may use the standard casino chips, more often than not, the casino will cash the player in and give him special roulette chips in a color that is exclusively his. The player must determine the amount each special chip is worth in the American game, while in the European game, the chips are usually predesignated and standard. In the American game, the casino will have a minimum that the chips must be worth (usually one dollar) but you can cash in and ask that each chip be worth $10, $20, or $100, etc. The casino will also have a table minimum bet and a table maximum bet. If the minimum bet is $5, you must place this amount as your wager, although you can bet on five numbers of one dollar each to achieve this — if one dollar is the minimum allowable chip designation. When you are betting on the numbers, you place your bet directly on the layout for that number. If someone else's bet is already there, you place your bet on top of his or hers. Since each player has different colored chips, the dealer is able to tell whose bet is whose in the event that number hits.

As the players are placing their bets, the dealer will spin the ball. As the ball rotates on the backtrack, players will continue to bet as they wish. However, at a certain point the dealer will wave his hand over the table and say: "No more bets." That signals the end of all betting and any bets placed after this will not count. Usually the dealer calls no more bets while the ball has four to six rotations to go before it descends into the slots. Once the decision is made, the dealer places a marker on the winning number, calls out the win and the color and collects all the losing bets. In America, the bets are collected by hand; in Europe they are raked in by a stick (similar to the stick in craps). The players are not allowed to place new bets while the marker is down. Once all the losing bets are collected, the dealer begins to pay the winning bets, still keeping the marker in place. When all the winning bets are paid, the dealer removes the marker and a new round of betting begins.

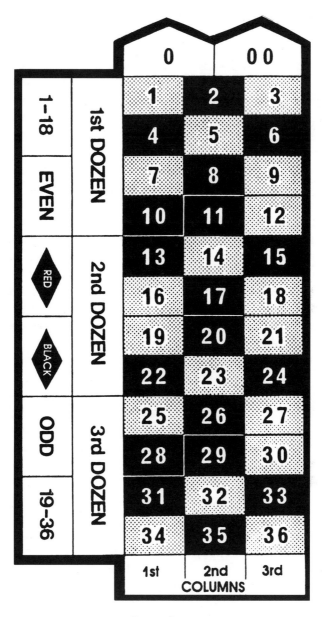

Figure One:
The American Roulette Layout

The Set Up of Roulette

The layout in *Figure One: The American Roulette Layout* is arranged in numerical order from left to right in columns of three, beginning with one, two, three and ending with 34, **35** and 36. The top of the layout has a *0* and a *00* if it is an American wheel, or *0* if it is a European wheel (sometimes called a French wheel). The American wheel is also called the *double-zero wheel* and the European wheel is also called the *single-zero wheel*. Strangely enough, the "European" or single-zero wheel was first developed and played in America and was subsequently brought to Europe where it caught on; while the "American" or double-zero wheel was a European invention which was brought to America. Thus, the European wheel is really an American wheel and the American wheel is actually a European wheel. As Macbeth said: "Nothing is but what is not." Nowhere is this statement more true than in gambling.

However, today, when you hear people talking about the European wheel, they always mean the single-zero variety, and when they talk about the American wheel, they always mean the double-zero device. For some bizarre reason, American gamblers have been content to play the double-zero wheel, which is an inherently inferior roulette game with a much greater house edge as we shall see, and even when given a choice in a casino between single- or double-zero roulette, they have stayed with the double zero. A big mistake, as you shall see.

Any bet placed directly on a number or on a line between numbers is called an *inside bet.* Any bet placed in the boxes and columns on the outside of the layout is called, appropriately enough, an *outside bet.* If you take a look at the wheels in *Figure Two: The American Roulette Wheel* and *Figure Three: The European Roulette Wheel*, you'll notice that neither wheel has much of a correlation with the layouts. The reason for this is simple. Not all roulette wheels are perfectly balanced, not all pockets are perfectly pitched, not all frets (the barriers between pockets) are equally stable, and some sections or numbers might tend to come up more often than other sections or numbers if the wheel is even slightly off. What causes a bias can be any of a number of things as stated. However, since most players are only interested in the betting areas, which are on the layout, and are not interested in the wheel, the casinos can protect themselves against someone stumbling on a hot number or section by making the pattern of numbers on the layout not correspond too closely with the pattern of numbers on the wheel. The layout player might enjoy betting groups of numbers but these groups exist only on the layout, not on the wheel. If you wanted to bet the numbers one, two, three, four, five and six on the layout, it would not be very hard since these numbers are all together. However, take a look at both the American and European wheels. The numbers one to six are spread out on the wheels. Although one to six form a continuous section of the layout, they do not form a continuous section of the wheel. The player betting those numbers would not be able to accidentally exploit a sector bias because those numbers don't represent a sector of the wheel. The casinos know that by positioning the numbers on the wheel as they do, players will not be inadvertently able to take advantage of a biased wheel.

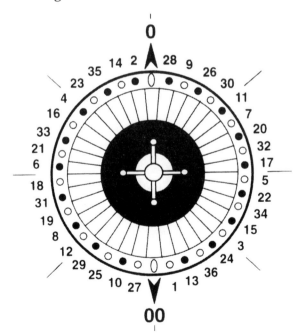

Figure Two:
The American Roulette Wheel
Taken from "Action Play Roulette Tracker" Card

Since most American casinos use the double-zero wheel, we shall analyze this model first. Take a look at the wheel in *Figure Two: The American Roulette Wheel.* The single zero *(0)* is on the top, the double zero *(00)* is directly across from it on the bottom. The numbers have been "righted" so that they are easily readable. The actual numbers on a roulette wheel all face in or out. Now, going clockwise, you will note the following:

1. There are 38 numbered grooves for the ball to fall into 1 through 36 and 0 and *00.*
2. Half the numbers are red (open "o" on diagram), half are black (black dot on diagram).
3. The *0* and the *00* are green (on rare occasions *0* and *00* are blue).
4. Almost directly across from each even number is the next odd number (and vice versa). Thus, 34 is almost directly across from **33** and **35** is almost directly across from 36. Note that the closest the layout comes to the wheel is in the positioning of 19 and 18, which are separated on the wheel by only one number — **31.**
5. Pairs of even numbers alternate with pairs of odd numbers except when split at the poles by *0* and *00.* The *0* splits the even numbers **2** and **28**; the *00* splits the odd numbers 27 and 1.
6. The colors of the numbers on the wheel correspond to the colors of the numbers on the layout, the only correspondence between layout and wheel. For inside play, the colors are irrelevant as the colors are irrelevant for all outside play except red-black.

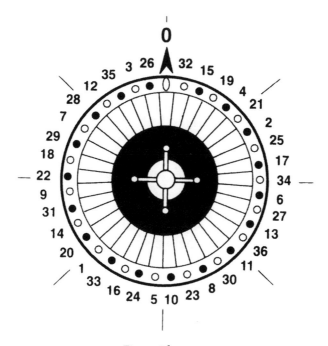

Figure Three:
The European Roulette Wheel
Taken from "Action Play Roulette Tracker" Card

The above is the European wheel which is slowly and thankfully making a comeback in America. You'll notice that while the wheel alternates the red and black and has 36 numbers ranging from one to 36 as does the American wheel, it has only one zero (in our diagram at the top). In Europe this zero is either green or blue. Thus, there are 37 possible spots for the ball to land, one fewer than the American wheel and, as we shall see, this makes for a better game.

The Percentages of Roulette

When you buy into a roulette game, the dealer will more than likely hand you one or more stacks of colored chips. In America, it is traditional for almost every player to have his or her own colored chips. This is to avoid the confusion so common in Europe where quite often players and dealers alike don't know whose bet is whose when it comes to payoff time. Thus, to avoid flaring tempers and flying fists, the casinos in America have decided to do away with the European same-chips tradition and give every player his or her own chips. While this individualism in chips might be a blow to colonialism, still the old world offers the better game, albeit with a little more confusion.

Once you have your chips, you have a host of bets to choose from. Like craps, roulette is a cornucopia of betting opportunities. Unfortunately, and with very few exceptions, most roulette bets give the casino a substantial 5.26 percent advantage at the double-zero American wheel and a 2.70 percent advantage on the single-zero European wheel. But it is possible to get that casino edge down to a comfortable 1.35 percent in certain roulette games as we shall see. However, first let's take a look at how the casinos are able to stack the roulette chips in their favor (I can never resist a pun).

On the double-zero wheel there are 38 possible decisions that can be rendered on a given spin of the ball (39 if you count the possibility of the ball flying off the wheel as it's spun and hitting a customer — an event I've seen happen on a number of occasions — unfortunately the casino will not book that bet!). The true probability of any one number hitting (*0* and *00* included) is one in 38. Thus, the *true* odds are 37 to one. You'll lose 37 times for every one time that you win. If the casino followed the true odds, then for every dollar that you bet on a number, when that number hit, you would receive $37 in return. This is called a *fair game* because neither the casino nor the player has the edge. Mathematically, a *fair* game results in a theoretical tie if played till the end of time. In the real world, of course, such a thing would not happen. Over the long run (millions of spins), the chances would be great that the player was somewhat ahead, the casino was somewhat ahead, or they were both *about* even. Naturally, in short-run play, say 38 spins, it would be almost unheard of for each number to come up only once (see Chapter Nine for the odds on oddball questions). In reality, some numbers would come up more than once, some numbers would not come up at all.

Most recreational players, no matter how often they go to

casinos, are in the game for the short run. The casinos are in the game for the long run and *expect* to make a good profit from their roulette games. To do this, the casinos must alter the payoffs on the winning bets so that even good luck will be too little to overcome good math. Here's how they do it.

In a fair game, if you bet one dollar on the 12 and it hit, you would receive a $37 payoff. In the real world of casino roulette, the payoff is not 37 to one but 35 to one. If your number wins, you are paid $35 and not $37. In essence, the casino took a tax of two dollars out of your win and kept it for itself. (That's also called the "vig" or "vigorish.") Now, what does that mean for the long-run playing of roulette? If you were to play 38 spins and each number hit its theoretical one time — you would win one bet and lose 37 bets but only be paid 35 to one on your winner. Thus, you would wind up losing two dollars. That constitutes a house edge of 5.26 percent. You simply take the total amount wagered, in this case $38 dollars (one dollar per spin) and divide it into what the house takes out of your win (in this case two dollars) and you come up with 5.26 percent (or 5.26315 percent to be exact). What does this mean in dollars and cents? Here's the awful truth. For every $100 you bet at roulette in the American double-zero wheel, you can expect to lose $5.26 in the long run. Not a good prospect.

Now, on the European single-zero wheel, the player has a better time of it. There are 37 numbers (the 0 included) and thus the probability of any one number hitting is one in 37. That makes for odds of 36 to one. However, the casino still pays 35 to one on the European wheel and thus the player is taxed one dollar for a win as opposed to a two dollar tax on the American wheel. This gives the casino a smaller edge of 2.70 (37 divided into one equals 2.7027 percent to be exact). Given a choice of the two games, you'd have to be foolish to play the American wheel if you had the possibility of playing the European one. So before you make your casino vacation plans, call the casinos and ask if they have single-zero roulette. Many American casinos now do. And all European casinos still do.

There are two exceptions to the 5.26 edge the casino has in the American double-zero game and one exception to the 2.70 percent in the European game. Both of these I will explain when I cover the various types of bets you can place in roulette. Since roulette is the quintessential European game, much of the language of roulette is French. Although the American game has removed much of the French flavor, those of you who will take cruises or play in casinos around the world will discover that the language of banking is also the language of roulette. Thus, in the following I shall give the English and French terms (when applicable) in parentheses for the various bets or propositions. For you Americans going to Europe, beware of the following: Since the players don't usually have individually colored chips, you have to keep a sharp eye on your bets and make sure that you are receiving the full payouts. There are quite a few roulette cheats who work the European casinos looking for unwary players and lazy *croupiers* (dealers) to hoodwink. Also, in Europe croupiers (dealers) expect to get a tip every time you win an inside bet. Some can get a little surly if you don't come forward with "their" share. Unfortunately, if you do tip after every inside win, you have voluntarily given up the reduced casino edge in this game to keep the staff civil. You'll have to decide how you want to handle this matter. I believe that players should tip dealers who give good service in a pleasant way but not tip in such a way that the player makes a good game a bad game by his generosity.

Some of the following bets have more than one term describing them.

Inside Bets

The Straight Up Bet
(French: En Plein)

You bet one or more numbers by placing your wager directly on the number or numbers you wish to wager. If your number or one of your numbers hits, you will be paid off at 35 to one. The house edge: Double-zero wheel = 5.26 percent. Single-zero wheel = 2.70 percent.

Split Bet
(French: A Cheval)

You place your wager on a line between two numbers. If either of these two numbers comes up, you are paid off at 17 to one. A split can also be made between 0 and 00 on the American wheel by placing a wager between them. However, if you are too far away to split the top 0 and 00, most casinos will accept a split of these numbers by placing your wager on the line between the Second Dozen Box and the Third Dozen Box. The house edge: Double-zero wheel = 5.26 percent. Single-zero wheel = 2.70 percent.

The Street Bet, or Three Number Bet, or "Side" Bet or the Trio
(French: Transversale)

This is a single bet on any one of three numbers hitting. You make this bet by placing your wager on the outside border of the three numbers you wish to bet on. If you win, you are paid off at 11 to one. The house edge: Double-zero wheel = 5.26 percent. Single-zero wheel = 2.70 percent.

The Corner, or Square or Four Number Bet
(French: Carre)

Here you are betting that one of four numbers will hit on the next spin. However, this wager can only be accepted on those numbers that form a square. You place your bet on the intersection where all four numbers meet. If you win, you are paid eight to one. The house edge: Double-zero wheel = 5.26 percent. Single-zero wheel = 2.70 percent.

The Five Number Bet

This bet only appears on the double-zero layout (thus it doesn't have a French equivalent) and is a single bet that one of the top five numbers (0, 00, 1, 2, or 3) will win on the next spin. You make this bet by placing your chips where the line between the 0 and the 3 meets the border of the layout. The bet pays off at six to one. This is one of the two bets on the

American double-zero wheel that carries an edge other than 5.26 percent. In this case, the player betting the "Five Number" has a staggering 7.89 percent disadvantage. This is the single worst bet in roulette. Some roulette writers call this bet "the beast with five numbers." It is monstrous indeed. If you want to bet these five numbers, you would be better off placing five separate bets, one for each number. That brings the house edge back down to 5.26 percent.

The Line Bet, or Six Number Bet or Sixline Bet (French: Sixain)

This bet is placed on the outside borders of the numbers at the line that separates the two sets of numbers. You are betting that one of those six numbers will hit on the next spin of the ball. This bet pays off at five to one. The house edge: Double-zero wheel = 5.26 percent. Single-zero wheel = 2.70 percent.

Outside Bets of Roulette

The Column Bet (French: Colonne)

This is a single bet that one of the columns of numbers on the layout will contain the number that hits. You place this bet at the bottom of the column in the area that says two to one. This wager pays off at two to one. The 0 and 00 are not considered a part of any column and thus the house has its usual advantage over the player. The house edge: Double-zero wheel = 5.26 percent. Single-zero wheel = 2.70 percent.

The Dozens Bet (French: Douzaine)

Here you are betting that within a dozen consecutive numbers on the layout, the lucky number will be hit. Keep in mind that this bet is not about a dozen consecutive numbers on the wheel. You make this bet in the areas labeled either First Dozen, Second Dozen or Third Dozen. If any one number in your dozens bet hits, you are paid off at two to one. The house edge: Double-zero wheel = 5.26 percent. Single-zero wheel = 2.70 percent.

The Odd and Even Bets
(French: Impair et Pair)

This bet is placed on the section of the layout that says, naturally enough, Odd or Even. There are 18 odd numbers and 18 even numbers on both the American double-zero wheel and the European single-zero wheel. There are therefore 18 ways to win and 20 ways to lose on the double-zero wheel and 18 ways to win and 19 ways to lose on the single-zero wheel. The bet pays off at even money. The house edge: Double-zero wheel = 5.26 percent. Single-zero wheel = 2.70 percent.

High or Low Bets
(French: Passe et Manque)

This bet is placed in the boxes marked either 1 to 18 or 19 to 36. It is a wager as to whether the high numbers or the low numbers will contain the winning hit. This is an even money bet and again there are 18 ways to win and 20 to lose on the double-zero wheel and 18 ways to win and 19 to lose on the single-zero wheel. The house edge: Double-zero wheel = 5.26 percent. Single-zero wheel = 2.70 percent.

Red or Black Bets
(French: Rouge et Noir)

The Red or Black is another even-money bet with the same winning chances as the Odd or Even bet above. This bet is placed on the area indicating red or black and is a wager that the winning number will be (you guessed it!) either a red one or a black one. The house edge: Double-zero wheel = 5.26 percent. Single-zero wheel = 2.70 percent.

It Pays to Surrender

In certain American double-zero games, it is possible to reduce the house edge on the even-money outside bets by taking advantage of an option called *surrender*. This option only exists on the Even-Odd, High-Low, or Red-Black bets — the so-called *even-money* bets. Some casinos will return half your bet if the 0 or 00 hits. Of course, the casino keeps the other half. This option effectively reduces the house edge in the double-zero game to 2.63 percent — not great, but twice as good as the normal 5.26 edge the casino enjoys on almost all of the other bets. If you are playing in a casino that has surrender then you are much better off wagering on the even-money bets. Often the casinos that have surrender don't advertise it. So ask: "Do you only take half the losing bet on the even-money propositions?" whenever you are playing in a new casino whose rules you're unsure of.

Being "En Prison" is Good!

The European single-zero wheel also has a variation that helps reduce the casino's edge on the even-money bets. This variation is called *en prison*. When the zero hits, all the bets on High-Low, Even-Odd, or Red-Black are imprisoned. They are not lost . . . yet. However, they cannot be won. Here's why. Once a bet is imprisoned, the player must wait for the next spin to "liberate" the bet or lose it. Let us say that you bet on black. The zero hit. You now must wait for another spin. If red hits again, you lose your black wager. However, if black hits, your wager is returned to you — it is liberated. You do not receive a win, you just get your money back. Should the zero hit while your bet is en prison, then it stays imprisoned for another spin and it takes two successive black hits to liberate the bet completely. Often European casinos will offer the player the option of losing half his bet rather than going through the en prison routine. I guess this is the European equivalent of plea bargaining. But it does reduce the casino's edge to a decent 1.35 percent which now makes it one of the better bets a bettor can make in a casino.

3

Layout Strategies and Systems

Grandma — generous, kind, loving, warm, happy, old-world and religious Grandma — always said to play the number six at roulette as it's a "working number" and anything over seven is "God's resting place." Grandma says those "working numbers" come in much more than the resting ones. So little Tim plays the number **6** in honor of Grams. His Aunt Grace, on the other hand, has twins — two lovely but somewhat slow-witted golden-haired boys — who were born on July 1, 1970 after 33 hours in labor. Grace likes to play the numbers 1, **2,** 7, 19 and **33** in honor of their existence (July is the "7"th month, she has **"2"** kids, born on the "1"st, in "19"70, after **"33"** hours in labor). Her brother, Fred, on the other hand, rues the day he married his wife, known in the neighborhood as Big Gert. He has had seven children with her; all of them have turned out to be indolent and shiftless and sour faced and *big*. Fred works like a dog and he's usually howling mad at the world. It was a black day when he asked Big Gert to marry him or so he says. He always bets his feelings . . . he bets black.

His best friend, Sam, has ESP and always looks for a sign or omen before he goes to a casino. The other day, he passed a billboard that said: "If it's an emergency call 911." So Sam bet 1, 9, **11,** and 19 - all the numbers that could be made with 911.

Of course, that scientific gambler, Sam's cousin Ed, knows that the above ways of playing are foolish and superstitious. I mean, Ed reads *Discover* magazine and he knows what he knows and he knows that there is one sure way to beat the casinos in roulette. His method is simple: he bets an even-money bet and after a loss, he doubles it. "Sooner or later I'm bound to win," he reasons. "It's the scientific law of averages. I only have to win one bet of a sequence to get all the money back that I lost." Not only that but Ed wins that first bet, too, if he wins at any stage in his progression. "I mean, how many times can a man lose an even-money bet in a row? The law of averages is on my side, right?" asks Ed.

His pal, Doug, eschews that way of thinking. Big deal. If Ed's bets win, he only wins one unit — that initial bet. Doug wants to make a killing. After a win, he parlays his winnings. He likes to bet whatever color (red or black) that last hit in the hopes of finding a trend. If he wins, he let's it all ride. He figures that colors get "hot" and he'll ride those hot colors into the economic sunset. Their third friend, Baldrick, has attempted to explain that the casino has a pretty big edge in roulette "because of the zeroes." So he bets Odd-Even and puts a small bet on both *0* and *00*. "That gives me 20 ways to win and 18 ways to lose. The odds favor me," Baldrick says triumphantly.

All the above scenarios have one thing in common. Sadly, except for a stroke of luck, none of the betting methods employed by our cast of characters can win in the long run. Not one of the methods outlined above can overcome the house edge of 5.26 on the double-zero wheel or 2.70 percent on the single-zero wheel. Because the house takes a tax out of your win — a pretty hefty tax by casino standards — the long-range prospects for the layout player are rather dim. Naturally on a given night, a given few days, perhaps even a given week, players can and do hit lucky streaks that defy the odds. If no one got lucky, no one would gamble (I think this is a true statement). This chapter is devoted to the various systems that have been developed to conquer Dame Fortune at roulette. I'll explain the system, explain how it works, why it will work most times, and why it will ultimately fail. Keep in mind that players who rely solely on luck, regardless of the system that they're playing, will eventually lose if the house has built in an edge. *And all casinos have built in an edge at roulette.* This is a terrible but true fact. So if you rely on luck remember this: Lady Luck is no lady. She is a whore who will sell her wares where and to whom she pleases or she'll just give her favors away even to the most unlikely or undeserving people. Remember this also as a case in point: one of the biggest Megabucks jackpots in slots was won by a man who was already a millionaire! Sitting next to him, at another machine, was a man who was living on his social security income. Lady Luck is fickle indeed and those in need are often shunned while she shines on those who don't need her light.

The Martingale System

Are you looking for a system that wins a majority of the time? Then look no further. The Martingale System, perhaps the oldest betting system ever devised, can give you a better than 99 percent chance of winning. In fact, the Martingale System on any given night is almost a sure winner. You can bet on that! Check the sentence before "You can bet on that!" and discover the single word that holds the key to the Martingale's wonder and its horror. Check the word "almost." Keep that word in mind as you read on.

The origin of the Martingale name is in some dispute. Some gaming researchers believe that it is a bastardization of the name Martindale and was named after Henry Martindale, a London casino owner in the 1700s. Other researchers believe that it is named after the mythological natives of Martin (or Gale) who bet this way in their primitive games or wore clothing that made them look foolish. Regardless of the name's origin, the Martingale System is one of the most played, least understood systems employed by first-time or novice gamblers and as such deserves some detailed attention. It is also the system most often sold by the hucksters of gambling as an "almost" surefire way to win!

The Martingale System is a double-up-after-you-lose system and it is probably the first system intelligent gamblers discover on their own when they contemplate ways to gain victory over the casinos. It is so logical, so elegant, so obvious that it just has to work! In fact, it was the first gambling system I ever used. And I "almost" won every time with it.

Let us say that you want to bet a dollar on a coin flip. You are betting that the next flip will be heads. You have a 50-50 chance of winning any given bet. Should you lose a bet, two bets, three bets, etc., you just keep doubling up until you finally win one. Here's the beauty of it. You only have to win one bet to be a winner! Here's how you employ the Martingale System.

Amount of Bet	Decision	Win	Loss	Total
$1	tails	——	$1	-$1
$2	tails	——	$2	-$3
$4	tails	——	$4	-$7
$8	tails	——	$8	-$15
$16	HEADS	$16	——	+$1

The above sequence of four losses in a row had a one in 16 chance of occurring. The true odds against it occurring were therefore 15 to one. That seems like a pretty safe bet, doesn't it? You'd only hit a losing streak of four straight tails once every 16 times you played. That's the good news of the Martingale System. At the outset the following chart shows you the odds of any given sequence of tails (or heads) happening. We are dealing in a strictly "fair" game where neither the casino nor the player has the edge. Here are the odds against various runs of a given bet (heads or tails) coming up in fair game.

Consecutive Hits	Probability	Odds Against-For
1	1 in 2	1 to 1
2	1 in 4	3 to 1
3	1 in 8	7 to 1
4	1 in 16	15 to 1

5	1 in 32	31 to 1
6	1 in 64	63 to 1
7	1 in 128	127 to 1
8	1 in 256	255 to 1
9	1 in 512	511 to 1
10	1 in 1,024	1,023 to 1

The mathematical formula for finding out the odds on a simple gambling proposition is relatively easy. Since the event has a one in two chance of happening (you'll either flip heads or tails, two possible decisions one of which you're betting on) you just multiply 2 x 2 however many times needed for the sequence. Thus, if you want to find out the probability for tails hitting, say, twice in a row just multiply 2 x 2 and you get a probability of once in four flips or odds of three to one against this happening. Say you want to find out how often tails will come up seven times in a row, just multiply 2 x 2 x 2 x 2 x 2 x 2 x 2 = 128. Thus, tails will hit seven times in a row once every 128 flips. The odds are therefore 127 to one. Tails hitting seven times in sequence will happen once and not happen 127 times. It is just such seemingly long odds that make the Martingale an alluring wager on even-money bets such as the flipping of a coin. Think about this: At the start of a Martingale progression that you are willing to take ten steps, the odds favor you by 1,023 to one! You will win your bet somewhere in that ten-step progression 1,023 times and only lose it once. The Martingale is still sounding pretty good, isn't it? "Almost" fool proof?

In point of fact, when we speak in terms of roulette it is a misnomer to talk of "even-money" bets and relate these to coin flipping. There are no true even-money bets in roulette. Yes, there are bets that pay even money but the odds are not 50-50 as in a coin toss. Let us take a look at the "even money" bets in roulette on both the double-zero wheel and the single-zero wheel. Keep in mind that on the double-zero wheel an "even-money" bet wins 18 times but loses 20 times. And on a single-zero wheel an "even-money" bet wins 18 times and loses 19 times. Thus, your chances of winning on a double-zero wheel are not one in two as in a coin flip but rather one in 2.11. Since the bet pays winners off at one dollar for every dollar bet instead of $1.11 for every dollar wagered, the house keeps 11 cents for itself — that casino tax again. This gives the house (you guessed it) a 5.26 percent advantage in the long run on "even-money" bets in the double-zero wheel. On a single-zero wheel the odds are one in 2.055 (rounded 2.06), which translates into a 2.70 percent advantage for the house in the long run.

Odds Against Consecutive Hits of "Even-Money" Roulette Bets (High-Low, Red-Black, Even-Odd)

Consecutive Hits	Double Zero Wheel Probability	Odds	Single Zero Wheel Probability	Odds
1	1 in 2.11	1.11 to 1	1 in 2.06	1.06 to 1
2	1 in 4.45	3.45 to 1	1 in 4.22	3.22 to 1
3	1 in 9.39	8.39 to 1	1 in 8.68	7.68 to 1
4	1 in 19.82	18.82 to 1	1 in 17.83	16.83 to 1
5	1 in 41.82	40.82 to 1	1 in 36.65	35.65 to 1
6	1 in 88.24	87.24 to 1	1 in 75.31	74.31 to 1
7	1 in 186.20	185.20 to 1	1 in 154.77	153.77 to 1
8	1 in 392.88	391.88 to 1	1 in 318.05	317.05 to 1
9	1 in 828.98	827.98 to 1	1 in 653.59	652.59 to 1
10	1 in 1,749.14	1,748.14 to 1	1 in 1,343.13	1,342.13 to 1

If you misread the above chart, you might think to yourself that betting against the consecutive proposition such as five blacks coming up in a row is a much better bet than is betting against five tails coming up in a row in a coin flip. On appearance it seems to be. However, appearances are deceiving. In reality, you are not betting one single bet that five blacks won't appear. Nor are you betting one bet that tails won't appear five times in a row. You are betting five separate bets, each double the amount of the last one, that your decision will appear. That point we'll take up shortly. But let's pretend that we are correct and five tails don't appear. When five tails fail to come up, a head invariably must come up and you win your Martingale progression. However, unlike a coin toss, in roulette when five blacks fail to come up, a red *does not* invariably come up. A *0* or *00* has a chance of showing up. This essentially means that you have to continue the Martingale progression because a *0* or *00* acts *as if* it's the other color. You can always think of the *0* or *00* as a wild card that acts against whatever "even-money" roulette bet you're attempting.

Now, let's look at why the Martingale Progression, while it wins frequently, is a long-run loser for the player. The "almost" is coming home to roost (to mix adjectives and aviaries).

Theoretically, the Martingale wager has to win eventually because the odds of, say, tails hitting, oh, a million times in a row are so large that I'm not even going to try to figure them. As long as you have enough money to keep doubling your wager, sooner or later you *must* win. True. However, notice that every casino you enter has a minimum and a maximum bet on every game and every table. You'll note that often that minimum and maximum bet allows only seven to nine doubling-up opportunities before the player is effectively frozen out of doubling up again.

Let's take a look at a casinos that have table minimum bets of $5 and maximum bets of $500 (more than likely), $1,000 (occasionally), and $2,000 (rarely) at a roulette table. Now, let's do our Martingale System and start at $5, which is one unit. Let's keep a record of how much we'll lose in aggregate as we go through our progression before we hit the casino's maximum bet of $500, $1,000, or $2,000.

Bet #	Units	Amount of Bet	Total Cumulative Loss
1	1	$5	$5
2	2	$10	$15
3	4	$20	$35
4	8	$40	$75
5	16	$80	$155
6	32	$160	$315
7	64	$320	$635
8	128	$640*	$1,275
9	256	$1,280*	$2,555
10	512	$2,560*	$5,115

Note that the progression ends on a $500 maximum table after seven doublings; at a $1,000 table after eight doublings, and at a $2,000 table after nine doublings.

How often can you expect to hit the 9th step in an even money progression? You'll hit it once every 512 times. How often in a ten-step? Once every 1,024 times. That's on a 1 to 1, or 50-50 proposition in a fair game. But you aren't in a 1 to 1 game. On the American wheel you're on a 1.11 to 1 and on the European wheel, you're on a 1.06 to 1. Of course, roulette is not paying you off at the correct odds of 2.11 to 1 or 2.06 to one, but rather at 1 to 1, making your economic outlook poor. The bottom line is simple. You will win an amazing number of decisions using the Martingale progression — "almost" all of them if you play in an extremely liberal casino that allows a $5 to $2,000 minimum to maximum spread (if you can find such a casino). But with each win, wherever it occurs in the progression, you will only win your minimum initial bet. (You get back all your previous losses plus that initial win.) However, when you lose the top bet on the last step — be it the 7th or 8th step as you'll find in most casinos or the 9th step as you'll find in extremely liberal casinos — your loss will be devastating. It will eat up all your wins and give the house its exact 5.26 or 2.70 percent edge. On the emotional side, think of how you would feel if on the next spin of the wheel, you were risking $1,280 to win $5. I don't think my heart could take that.

The other disconcerting thing about the Martingale progression is that your devastating loss could come at any time. You don't necessarily win 1,023 decisions before you lose number 1,024 in a ten-step. You might lose ten double-up wagers in a row the very first time you try the Martingale. More realistically, because most casinos won't tolerate a ten-step, you could lose a seven-step early and more often. Rather than give you math, let me give you an exercise. Just tour a casino that has many roulette tables with scoreboards that record the last 16 or 20 numbers that have hit. Note how many times seven consecutive odds, or evens, or reds or blacks, or highs or lows have come up. While this doesn't happen often, you'll probably see one or two in a short tour of a decent-sized casino. Now, think about the bundle you would have lost had you gone the full Martingale Progression on any of them. And think about your heart.

The common fallacy of the Martingale System is that you are betting against a long-shot. If you were betting only one bet that seven or eight or nine or ten sequences of black won't appear and getting paid even money for the bet if you won, you would be a rich, rich person in a very short, short period of time. But the Martingale is not one bet at the start of a series. It's not a bet about a series at all. It is seven or eight or nine individual and independent bets placed in succession on a 50-50 (or rather a 1.11 to 1 or 1.06 to 1) proposition. Each time that ball heads for a pocket, it's a whole new game because on an unbiased wheel each spin is an independent event. The most repeats of an even-money decision that I ever personally witnessed were 14 blacks in a row. Despite such an unlikely run, the fact that red came up on the 15th spin was still a 1.11 to 1 proposition.

Does the above cautionary information absolutely forbid you from using a Martingale-type system for a short run? No. Indeed, if you are interested in having your cake and eating it too, there is a type of Martingale that can actually decrease your overall economic risk. However, before getting into that, let us look at some other systems that have been employed at roulette.

The Grand Martingale System

There is a second type of Martingale System that bettors enjoy using called the Grand Martingale. In truth, the only thing grand about this system is that you'll lose your grand that much faster when you play it. That's because the Grand Martingale calls for a doubling of the previous bet *plus one unit*. Let us say that we are going to bet on red and every time black/green comes up we go into our progression. We double the previous bet and add one unit to it. Our minimum bet is $5. If we lost the first bet, the second bet would be double ($10) plus one unit ($5) which would be $15. We'll take the progression nine steps. Here's how it goes:

Bet #	Unit	Bet Amount	Decision	Win	Loss	Total
1	1	$5	black	——	$5	-$5
2	3	$15	black	——	$15	-$20
3	7	$35	black	——	$35	-$55
4	15	$75	black	——	$75	-$130
5	31	$155	black	——	$155	-$285
6	63	$315	black	——	$315	-$600
7	127	$635*	black	——	$635	-$1235
8	255	$1275*	black	——	$1275	-$2510
9	511	$2555*	black	——	$2555	-$5065

On the Grand Martingale, you'll note that we can only go six steps in a casino with a $500 maximum bet, seven steps in a casino with a $1,000 maximum bet, and eight steps in a casino that allows a $2,000 maximum bet. So, why would anyone play a Grand Martingale? Because when you win, you win more than just the initial bet. The Grand Martingale player is looking to score a bigger win as the progression advances. Notice that on the second step, the Grand Martingale player will win $10 if red appears, not $5 as would a regular Martingale player. With each step (until the awful and inevitable end) the Grand Martingale player reaps a greater reward for his greater risk.

There are other variations to the Grand Martingale family of wagers. For example, you can increase your bets as follows: 1 unit, 3 units, 8 units, 24 units, 50 units, 100 units. For a $5 minimum bet that would be six steps if the maximum bet were $500. Let's take a look at the steps and see what we would have won or lost had we stopped after a win or loss at each point for this particular variation of the Grand Martingale. Keep in mind that if you win the first bet, you would not go on to the second step; if you won the second step, you would not go on to the third and so forth.

Bet #	Units	Bet Amount	Stop/Win	Stop/Loss
1	1	$5	+$5	-$5
2	3	$15	+$10	-$20
3	8	$40	+$20	-$60
4	24	$120	+$60	-$180
5	50	$250	+$70	-$430
6	100	$500	+$70	-$930

It is obvious that if the Martingale is a dangerous system, the Grand Martingale and its variations are even more deadly. They are not a good long-range way to play. There is also this to consider. When a hot streak occurs, as they do, the Martingale or Grand Martingale player is making minimum bets. He is not looking to increase his bets after a win. But when a cold streak occurs, he is escalating his bets precipitously. Of course, in the long run, it doesn't matter what betting system a player uses in an unbiased roulette game, the results will be the same — the casino will maintain its edge and the player will lose. Betting systems merely redistribute the pattern of the wins and losses, not the final amounts.

The Labouchere System

This is a nice-sounding name for a rather poor playing system whose popularity waxes and wanes over the years as new players discover it (usually through a system seller promising huge wins), play it, lose with it, and then discard it. The system was first "discovered" by Henry Labouchere the famous English gambler who traveled the world playing it and who died in 1912. What he "discovered" was actually a system devised by the French mathematician, the Marquis de Cordorcet who lived in the 18th century. The Labouchere is a cancellation system. You take a row or column of numbers of a given length, for our example, let us say five: 1, 2, 3, 4, 5. Each number represents a unit(s) of betting. The first bet is a combination of the first and last numbers in the row. That would be six as 1+5 = 6. Each time you lose a bet, you write the amount at the end of the row or column. So, now we have 1, 2, 3, 4, 5, 6. Each time you win a bet, you cross out the first and last numbers in your column: 1̶, 2, 3, 4, 5̶. The next bet is again the combination of the first and last uncancelled numbers in the row or column. You keep playing until you have cancelled all the numbers. The theory is that you will win the total amount of your combined numbers in the first sequence at some point before you cancel out every number — in our case 1, 2, 3, 4, 5 = 15.

The Labouchere system is similar to the Martingale because it will result in a lot of little wins — "almost" all your sessions will in fact be winners. However, at some point in the cancellation process of a given session (THE SESSION FROM HELL), you will lose all the bets in the sequence, start a new sequence, lose all those, start a new sequence, lose those, then perhaps again, and perhaps again and finally hit the house limit.

The d'Alembert Betting System

The French mathematician Jean Le Rond d'Alembert formulated a theory of equilibrium postulated as follows: Given two events with an equal chance of happening, (our classic coin flipping of heads or tails) if one event begins to dominate, the other event must dominate in the future in order for equilibrium to be restored. His thesis was that nature tends towards equilibrium. So if heads has come up an inordinate number of times, you should start betting tails because it is destined to come up with greater frequency in the future for equilibrium to be established. What players who use this kind of thinking fail to realize is another simple principle, developed by me, called: *There Ain't Enough Time in World, Buddy, for Equilibrium.* Given a 50-50 proposition such as a coin flip, the theory goes that after millions of flips, you'll *probably* have 50 percent heads and 50 percent tails. I would be willing to bet that after a million flips, however, you would *definitely not* have *exactly* 500,000 heads and 500,000 tails. After a hundred flips, you might have heads come up 55 times, which is 55 percent of the time, and tails come up 45 times or 45 percent of the time. That's a pretty big percentage difference. But the difference in betting is only ten units won or lost depending on whether you are betting heads or tails. Now, as the number of trials progresses, you will see streaks of heads or tails, and after a million flips, you might find yourself with 499,300 heads and 500,700 tails — in terms of a percentage that is just about 50-50. But, had you been betting on heads, you would have lost 1,400 units — a goodly sum. Thus, equilibrium is only a theoretical ideal. Reality is its shadow effect.

The d'Alembert betting system is based on the assumption of equilibrium. The player of this system subtracts a chip after each winning bet, since a losing bet is more likely to come up next in order to establish equilibrium. The player adds a chip to any losing bet since a winning bet is more likely to come up next for the same reason. Thus, the player is attempting to capitalize on the "law" of equilibrium. At the end of a sequence, when equilibrium has been reached, the player will be up one unit. Of course, we know, based on a theory called "the maturity of chances," that equilibrium is essentially a mathematical construct. Take our example above. In the real world, the actual number of heads and tails hit on a million flips is much farther apart than it was after the first hundred flips (ten to 1,400) but the ratio (55 - 45 percent and 50.07 - 49.93 percent) was closer together. Again the problem with this system is that a losing streak which calls for a slight escalation of bets will make it that much more difficult to regain your money, since every time you win, you are decreasing your bets. In the end, the d'Alembert will give you a number of smaller winning sessions and a few big losing sessions.

Follow the Trend

Gambling is streaky in nature — no one would argue that. Any detailed or long-range look at any series of events (coin flips, red-black in roulette, etc.) shows that streaks can and will occur. Some of these streaks are dramatic, some short lived. Indeed, a pattern can be discerned in any prolonged series of events. Being pattern-finding creatures, we humans note the patterns of past events, analyze the patterns (perhaps even create a pattern or two) and then make a fundamental mistake — we project that pattern into the future. If a series of events is based on randomness, any patterns that develop are strictly fluctuations in that randomness. In a coin flip, if 10 heads have come up in a row, that doesn't mean that tails is more likely to come up next or that heads is more likely to continue streaking. The next flip is still a 50-50 proposition.

Tails has a one in two chance of coming up and heads has a one in two chance of coming up. Many gamblers, because they have seen those 10 heads come up just before, will bet the trend. Other gamblers will go against the trend. The fact is that in the long-run, the odds don't change no matter what the trend is in the short-run. Trend-finding systems are also sold as surefire winners and in a 50-50 proposition they win as often as not (but of course!).

For the roulette player playing an unbiased wheel, no betting system can overcome the long-range casino advantage as we have seen. Does that mean that the layout player is doomed to lose on a given night? No. In fact, systems players, as shown, will more often win than lose. If you like playing roulette but you intend to be a layout player, there are ways to apply various systems in such a way to reduce your overall risk and increase your overall pleasure. When you decrease risk, you decrease the amount of money you will theoretically lose in the long run (assuming you don't increase your playing time) or you will increase the amount of time you can play in a casino without increasing the amount of theoretical loss. Which leads us to the next chapter.

4

Increase Pleasure — Decrease Risk:

The Epicurean "Gland" Martingale and the "Adrenotrend" Systems for Outside Bets in Roulette

The sad fact that no betting system can ever hope to overcome the odds on an unbiased wheel in the long run will cause three reactions in players. The first is the *"No more roulette for me, I'll look into more player-friendly games like blackjack"* reaction. The second is the *"Well, tell me about strategies that deal with biased or potentially biased wheels or some other way to maybe overcome the odds"* reaction. And the third is the *"Frankly, my dear, I don't give a damn, I'm still going to play roulette"* reaction.

This chapter is for you Rhett.

If you are still interested in tackling roulette after reading the scare chapter that preceded this, I have some good news for you. Since most players only go to casinos occasionally such as once a month, once every two months, once a year, or such, the fact is that you aren't doomed to lose on those visits because the casino has the edge. This isn't a Greek tragedy where fate dictates the short-term as well as the long-term events. It's more a Shakespearean tragedy where you can profit in the short-term by your decisions, while still recognizing that in the long-

term, you are facing the abyss. And the really good news is
that you can increase your pleasure, and decrease your risk
while making occasional forays into the glitter domes of
Dame Fortune by following two basic systems of play for
outside bets.

The first I call the *Gland Martingale* system because it is
a variation of the Martingale wagering system that I discussed in Chapter Three. If I am correct in my assumption
that many people gamble on roulette because of the pleasure
they receive in anticipating the next decision then the *Gland*
Martingale takes this important factor into account — by
manipulating your adrenal glands. Essentially what you will
do is practice various Martingale and anti-Martingale (or
trend-spotting) systems by *waiting* a set number of decisions
before risking your money. Waiting will cause your adrenaline to pump as you anticipate a betting opportunity —
that's why these trend-spotting systems are lumped under
the heading "Adrenotrends." While all this heart-pumping is
happening, your money is not at risk. You receive at once the
pleasure of gaming, which is partly in the anticipation, with
none of the attendant risk. There are various ways to approach the Gland Martingale and Adrenotrend systems, depending upon how much anticipation you want and how
much risk. I am going to divide my systems into two broad
types: a five-step Gland and an in-and-out Adrenotrend.
Each system can be played in a stationary way at one table
or in a wandering way with the player going from table to
table. For each system, I will give you a minimum number of
units needed to play the system through one cycle. A cycle is
defined *negatively* as: how much you need if you get clobbered and lose every bet! At the end of my discussion, I am
going to set some ground rules that will guarantee that you
are *actually* decreasing risk as opposed to *apparently* decreasing risk. Will any of these systems diminish the odds that the
casino has over you? No. But all will decrease the total
amount you can expect to lose in your playing sessions and
in the long run. The only work you'll have to do is keep a
short-term record of the even-money hits that you have decided to track if the casino where you are playing doesn't
have a scoreboard that records such things for you. For the

purposes of our discussion, I will focus on the outside bets of red-black. But all the bets that are even-money can be substituted for red-black.

The Gland Martingale

This is a strategy to maximally maximize anticipation and maximally minimize risk. You will find that you will not be getting into the action all that often and when you do, you won't be staying in the action for very long. You'll need three units for this Martingale. Wait for five reds or blacks to appear and then bet one unit on the opposite color. If you lose double your bet. If you lose again, quit and wait for five more of a given color to appear before doing this two step once again.

Let's look at it.

You come to the table and record the following (all these examples have been taken from actual scoreboards I've recorded): R, **B**, *0*, R, R, R, **B, B, B, B, B.** Now you bet one unit on red. If you win, you are up one unit and you wait until five blacks or reds hit again. However, if you lose, you double the bet.

Let us say you lost, that black came up again and then again. You're out three units. Picking up the sequence: **B, B,** (lost 3 units) R, R, **B**, R, *00*, R, R, R, **B**, *00*, **B**, R, R, R, **B, B, B,** R, R, R, R, R, (bet 1 unit) **B** (won 1 unit on black).

Now how has this system increased your pleasure but minimized your risk? Well, there were 36 decisions recorded. You were there for all 36 decisions, waiting patiently, all the while building that anticipatory set — in short, your adrenaline was pumping. Let us assume that your unit bet is $10. You had a total of $40 at risk for 36 spins ($10 + $10 +$20). Forget whether you won or lost in a given sequence because we want to view the totality of the experience. In the math of gambling the casino edge can be figured on the total amount wagered. That's why I'll often write that in the long run for every $100 bet you will lose "X" amount; "X" being the casino edge translated into money. So for every $100 bet at the American double-zero roulette game, the house will win $5.26 because its edge is 5.26

percent. The casino has a 5.26 percent edge on that $40 (in the long run). So for every $40 you bet, you will lose approximately $2.10 (rounding down). Had you been playing every spin during that time frame, you would have bet $360 which is nine times as much. You would theoretically have lost nine times as much or approximately $18.94 (rounding up) during that same time period. The increase in pleasure occurred as you waited (and maybe waited and waited and waited) for the proper betting moment. By the time five of any color hits, you've got to be pretty pumped up and ready to get into the action.

In point of fact, for many players the above Gland Martingale might not increase pleasure enough to overcome the boredom that might develop in waiting and waiting and waiting. For you, consider using the *wandering* version of the Gland Martingale. This version is also called "Rocco's Roulette" in honor of my Uncle Rocco who has done quite nicely with it on his monthly bus trips to Atlantic City. This system can only be played in casinos that have scoreboards.

You are still going to look for five straight hits of either red or black before betting the opposite. You are still only doing a two-step Martingale. However, instead of staying at one table, you are going move around and look at the scoreboards. In some casinos, you will have many more betting opportunities because there are many more scoreboards. Here are 10 scoreboards from the same casino. Each scoreboard recorded 20 hits. Note how often you would have been in the action. Remember that the roulette scoreboards add the new number *to the top* and not the bottom. They should be read from bottom to the top as the arrow indicates. Thus, on the first column, the last color to hit was R.

1	2	3	4	5	6	7	8	9	10
R	R	B	R	R	B	R	R	B	B
R	B	R	B	B	0	R	R	R	R
B	R	B	B	R	B	B	B	R	R
B	R	B	R	B	B	R	B	R	B
R	B	R	0	B	B	R	R	B	B
R	B	R	R	R	B	R	R	R	B
R	R	R	B	R	R	R	B	B	R
B	R	R	00	B	B	R	R	B	R
B	B	R	R	B	B	R	B	R	R
R	B	B	R	R	B	R	R	B	R
R	R	B	B	B	R	B	B	B	R
R	B	0	B	R	R	B	R	R	B
B	00	R	B	B	B	B	R	B	B
B	B	R	B	B	R	R	R	B	R
R	R	B	B	R	R	B	B	B	B
B	B	B	B	B	R	00	B	0	B
R	B	B	00	R	B	00	R	B	R
R	B	B	B	R	B	0	R	B	B
B	B	B	B	R	B	R	B	R	R
R	B	B	R	R	R	R	0	B	B

If we go up the columns, we will note the following:

Column 1: No betting opportunities. Total: 0 units.

Column 2: Five blacks appeared, followed by a red. Total: +1 unit.

Column 3: Six blacks in a row. We would have lost one unit after the first five blacks but won two units after the sixth black because red appeared, for a win of one unit. Further up, we see five reds hitting in a row, followed by a black for a win of one unit. We won two units in column three. Total: +3 units.

Column 4: Six blacks in a row. We would have lost one unit after the first five blacks but won two units after the sixth black because red appeared, for a win of one unit.
Total: +4 units.

Column 5: No betting opportunities. Total: +4 units.

Column 6: No betting opportunities. Total: +4 units.

Column 7: Seven reds in a row. Lost one unit after the

fifth red, and then two units after the sixth red. We lost our maximum three units on this and stopped the progression. Total: +1 unit.
Column 8: No betting opportunities. Total +1 unit.
Column 9: No betting opportunities. Total +1 unit.
Column 10: Five reds in a row followed by a black. Win one unit. Total: +2 units.

We risked a total of 12 units over the course of 200 decisions on 10 different wheels. If we were betting $10 as our unit, we would have put $120 into action. On this particular set of hits, we are ahead $20. The casino's theoretical take in the long run on $120 would be $6.31. What if we had played all 200 spins — albeit an impossibility for one person but someone had to be playing those spins — what would be our expectation? We would have put into action $2,000 from which the casino's theoretical take would be $105.20.

If you look at the ten columns of hits, you will note that had you decided to be more daring and go with a four-hit pattern, you would have had more betting opportunities. The Gland Martingale can be employed this way also — with one caveat. You are putting more total money at risk and, keep in mind, the casino edge works on every dollar put into action. Still, if the five-step Gland doesn't give you the anticipatory rush you need, go with a four-stepper. Do not go with a three-step because at this stage, you are risking too much money in the long run. If you are going to be a layout player, your primary motivation is to reduce risk. The Gland Martingale certainly does this. And if you decide to employ my Uncle Rocco's variation and wander around, you'll get a little exercise in to boot.

Adrenotrends

This is a hot and cold system that hopes to exploit runs of the same type (reds, blacks, odds, evens, highs, lows). Once again, we want to add the joy of anticipation while diminishing the casino's overall take on us. We do this by cutting in half the total number of decisions we're involved in. All adrenotrends are one-off-one-up-and-out betting schemes. You will go to your table. Whatever color was the last to hit, you will bet that color. That's it. You either win or lose that bet. Then you wait for the next hit without betting, whatever color that is, you bet one unit on a repeat. This system is good for stationary playing and for wandering. It reduces your total exposure approximately in half because you are only betting on half the decisions. (You could make a case that wandering might give you more risk time. It might. That all depends on how fast you walk.)

If we look at the ten columns and use these as our base, here's what we notice. Again we read down to up. We ignore 0 and 00. They are non-events. Except if they hit on one of our bets, then we lose and wait for the next color before going back in.

Column 1:   Total units risked: 10. Won 4 units. Total: +4 units.
Column 2:   Total units risked: 10. Push.   Total: +4 units.
Column 3:   Total units risked: 9.   Won 5 units. Total: +9 units.
Column 4:   Total units risked: 9.   Lost 1 unit. Total: +8 units.
Column 5:   Total units risked: 10. Lost 4 units. Total: +4 units.
Column 6:   Total units risked: 9.   Won 3 units. Total: +7 units.
Column 7:   Total units risked: 8.   Won 2 units. Total: +9 units.
Column 8:   Total units risked: 9.   Lost 7 units. Total: +2 units.
Column 9:   Total units risked: 9.   Lost 1 unit. Total: +1 unit.
Column 10:   Total units risked: 10. Lost 2 units. Total: -1 unit.

Remember that we won our last example (by a little) and now we lost this example (by a little). Let us look at the overall picture. We risked 93 units, as opposed to 200 units had we bet on every spin. If we are using $10 as our unit, we put $930 into action. The theoretical casino edge would have been $48.92 as opposed to $105.20 for the entire 200 spins, which translates into $2,000 of our money in action. Unfortunately, we lost a unit, which means we lost $10. However, this adrenotrend system clearly shows that the total risk has been reduced substantially, yet you are still getting all the benefits of that nice adrenaline rush as you wait to place your bets.

What if You Must Play Every Spin?

Some casinos, especially on busy weekends, insist that to have a seat at a roulette table, the player must play every spin. If you are a player who bets fairly substantial sums, you can employ the Gland Martingale by making table minimum bets on every spin and when five reds or blacks (or other even-money bets) appear in a row going to your normal full-size bet. The casino will be chopping away at those small bets with its edge but if they are a tiny fraction of your regular wager, the damage will not be that great. However, if you are a minimum wagerer, then you'll have to stand and/or wander or convince the pit boss that you have a condition that absolutely makes it necessary for you to sit. Apropos of this, there is one roulette player I know who asks for a wheelchair when he visits the casino. He makes some excuse about a twisted ankle or whatever, gets the casino to supply him with a wheelchair, and plays his Gland Martingale (he calls it: "My negative fiver") to his heart's content from his seat.

Establishing Veracity and Bankroll Requirements

If you are playing the layout, you can make variations of your own on the ideas I have presented in this chapter. What you want to establish is a method for consistently reducing your exposure to the casino's driving edge in roulette. Let us say that on a typical weekend, you plan to put in four hours of play a day — an amount of time that many people play. If you use the Gland Martingale system, you will still only play for those four hours but you will have reduced your risk considerably. If you use the Adrenotrends as your system, you will have reduced your risk approximately in half. With both systems of play, you are still getting the full anticipatory joy of the game, without the full economic risk.

The other way to approach the Gland Martingale system is to give yourself a predetermined number of decisions that you'll watch — either on various scoreboards or at one table.

Obviously, if you gave yourself 500 decisions, you would be finished much faster by employing Rocco's wandering variation than if you sat for 500 decisions at one table. In either case, go in with a predetermined plan. If you use the probability chart on page 32, you can see that if you were to give yourself 500 decisions (on a single wheel this would be five to seven hours of play), you would get into the action approximately 12 times on a double-zero wheel and approximately 14 times on a single-zero wheel during this span. If you wanted more action for your 500 decisions, you could do a four-step Gland Martingale. In that case you would theoretically get into the action 25 times on a double-zero wheel and 28 times on a single-zero wheel. The reason you get into the action more on the single-zero wheel is because only that lone zero will interrupt runs of even-money decisions. Thus, there is a greater chance for runs in single-zero roulette than in double-zero roulette. In either case, by playing the Gland Martingale your long-term prospects are much better than if you had wagered on each of those 500 spins.

How much money do you need to play the Gland Martingale and the Adrenotrends systems? Looking disaster squarely in the face, you should have enough money to weather an epic storm and be able to come back the next day. You should have the required units for every single spin you will theoretically play. For the Adrenotrend system, just take half of the number of decisions you intend to play. For 500 decisions, that's 250 units. For the Gland Martingale, if you are playing 12 times on a double-zero wheel, it is possible that you will have to risk three units each time (one unit after the first five, two units if you lost that bet) and you may lose three units each time — for a total of 36 units. So 36 units should be your single-day stake to play the five-step Gland Martingale on a double-zero wheel. The following chart will give you a good idea of what it requires to play the Gland Martingale system in such a way that you are guaranteed to last. If you are going to play for a weekend or three days, these single-day amounts would probably see you through with very little chance of your actually being wiped out. This chart is based on 500 decisions of the Gland Martingale

Wheel Type	4-Step	5-Step
Single Zero	84 units	41 units
Double Zero	76 units	36 units

The next chart translates units into money for the Gland Martingale. This is how much money you would need to bring in order to play the Gland Martingale given a basic monetary unit.

Single Zero	$2	$3	$5	$10	$15	$20	$25	$50
4-Step	$168	$252	$420	$840	$1,260	$1,680	$2,100	$4,200
5-Step	$82	$123	$205	$410	$615	$820	$1,025	$2,050

Double Zero	$2	$3	$5	$10	$15	$20	$25	$50
4-Step	$152	$228	$380	$760	$1,140	$1,520	$1,900	$3,800
5-Step	$72	$108	$180	$360	$540	$720	$900	$1,800

For those of you lucky enough to play a single-zero wheel with *en prison,* or the double-zero wheel with surrender, your expected overall loss will be a little less since you'll only lose one-half of your bet when the *0* or *00* shows after five reds or five blacks.

The Gland Martingale on Columns and Dozens

The Gland Martingale system can also be employed on other outside bets. For example, let us take a look at the Dozens and Columns bet. On the Dozens, you are betting that a certain 12 numbers (First Dozen = 1-12; Second Dozen = **13-24**; Third Dozen = 25-36) will hit on the next round. The Columns are a dozen diverse numbers (First Column = 1,**4**,7, etc.; Second Column = **2**, 5, **8, 11**, etc.; Third Column = 3, **6**, 9, 12, etc.) that run the length of the layout. Instead of a one in 2.11 or one in 1.06 chance on the double-zero and single-zero wheels respectively on the even-money bets, you have a one in 3.17 chance of hitting any dozen numbers on a double-zero wheel and a one in 3.08 chance of hitting any dozen on a single-zero wheel. The casino makes its money on these bets (as usual) because it does not pay you the true odds of 2.17 and 2.08 to one when you win. Instead, the casino pays off at two to one — which again translates into the respective edges of 5.26 and 2.70 percent on double and single-zero wheels. An astute gambler might think he is helping his cause by putting up an extra bet on the 0 and 00 to cover that possibility and "protect" his other bets, but this does not enhance the chances of bringing home the money. Since both the 0 and 00 also have a tax extracted on a win, you are not cutting down the casino's edge one bit. Instead, you are offering up still more money for that edge to cut into. The best way to play a Gland Martingale on the Columns and Dozens is to wait five or six decisions where one Dozen or one Column does not appear. Then bet one unit on that column. If you win, you wait for another five or six decisions where once again a particular Dozen or Column doesn't appear. However, if you lose, you bet another unit. If you should win this second bet, you are ahead because the bet pays off at two to one. However, if you should lose the second bet also, you would now increase your bet to two units. Win or lose that third bet is the end of the Gland Martingale for this type of bet.

One last word and it's almost a refrain. No layout system can overcome the edge. Period. The Gland Martingale and the Adrenotrends systems simply extend your time and not your risk. Even after five hits of a given color the odds are still 1.11 to one that either red or black will appear on the next spin in double-zero and 1.06 to one in single-zero. For a Dozen or Column bet the odds are still 2.17 and 2.08 to one on double-zero and single-zero wheels respectively. It doesn't matter what happened on the previous decision or the previous ten decisions. So why not just happily throw out your money on all spins and patterns be damned? Because the more money you throw out, the better shot the casino has at it. The player's best chance in a game with a negative expectancy is the short run since almost anything can happen in a controlled number of decisions. My two systems of play simply take the short-run and extend it over time. However, over the long haul — whatever that long haul is — the casino will get its cut from your bets, no matter what system you use. Thus, the less you bet overall, the less you lose. That's the awful truth. But you are still getting the excitement of anticipation by waiting a bit before you plunge in. That's the wonderful truth.

Still, there is much more to understanding roulette than just throwing up our hands in defeat and exclaiming: "I can't beat this game!" Because that statement is not true. There are approaches, both long-term and short-term, that definitely can give you a good shot at beating the casinos in roulette. Do you really want a shot at beating the wheel? Then, you have to do just that, you have to *beat the wheel* and that is the subject of our next chapter.

5

Golden Numbers:

How to Beat the Wheel
in Roulette

Theoretically, roulette is an unbeatable game *if* the mechanism of the roulette wheel is flawlessly balanced, *if* the pockets are uniformly structured and surfaced, *if* the frets have the same resiliency, *if* the dealers are incapable of controlling consciously or unconsciously the fall of the ball, and *if* the players are unable to anticipate by sight where the ball will land. Those are quite a few *ifs* and because of them roulette has given rise to several wonderful strategies designed to exploit potentially beatable *wheels.* I stress the word "wheels" because to win at roulette you must either beat the mechanism itself or the dealer who controls the ball. You cannot beat the *theoretical structure* of roulette as you can beat the structure of blackjack with card counting, but you can beat the *physical practice* of roulette, as you can beat the physical practice of craps if you can control the dice. In theory roulette is unbeatable but in the real world factors exist that prevent the theory from being executed with perfect precision. Just as the best-running cars have occasional mechanical problems, so too do roulette wheels. Roulette wheels are physical mechanisms made up of parts, of wood and metal, and like all physical mechanisms, they can wear out, get "gremlins," and function imperfectly. And they wear out inconsistently — a little here, a little there. Just like a car that falls apart part by part, so does a roulette wheel.

In addition, people and machines coexist in a relationship where one or the other will occasionally make "mistakes" or malfunction. Pilot error in an air crash. Engine failure. Just as some drivers of cars get into certain driving patterns, so perhaps do roulette dealers. To beat roulette, you must beat either man or machine, perhaps both. The layout, the bets and the betting systems I've discussed previously are irrelevant to your long-run chances of victory. My layout strategies simply reduce overall risk by reducing your total action. They cannot bring you the gold from the casinos. The layout is merely where you place your bets. The only betting "system" that is guaranteed to win is betting on a *favorable occurrence* and having the money to back yourself. This is called advantaged play because you, the player, have the odds in your favor. So it's wheelers and dealers and then, you can spin roulette gold. I'll deal with wheels in this chapter and in Chapter Seven I'll deal with dealers and other methods of getting the edge.

Biased Wheel Play

The best (and safest) system for beating the wheel is to record a sufficient number of decisions to ascertain whether any one number, or group of numbers or sector of the wheel is biased, then bet that number, or group of numbers or sector. A biased wheel is defined as a wheel where one or some numbers are hitting with greater-than-average expectancy. If we use the American double-zero wheel as our model, in 38 spins of the wheel each number has a theoretically equal chance of coming up once. Naturally, in 38 spins, anything will happen. For the purposes of biased-wheel play 38 spins is merely a drop in probability's bucket. For biased-wheel play, you have to analyze the bucket.

Let us take an absurd example as a case in point. If there were some glue in a pocket (say number **8**) and every time the ball hit that pocket, it stayed, then there's a good chance that **8** would come up once every five to ten spins. Let's make it once every ten spins. If you analyzed 1,000 decisions of the wheel and you noticed that **8** had come up a hundred times, you would start betting on **8** for every spin thereafter. Since the casino pays you 35 to one for every winning hit on a number, had you bet one dollar, you would lose $9 but win $35 on every ten spins of the wheel for a net gain of $26 per ten spins. In short order, you would be a millionaire because as your bankroll increased, you would naturally increase the size of your bets.

The chance of finding a biased wheel where a number — any number — was coming up once every ten times is understatedly remote. However, for a player to win money at roulette in the long haul, a bias does not have to be quite so pronounced. Indeed, the key elements in beating the wheel are threefold:

1. that the bias be real and not imagined.
2. that the bias be sufficient to overcome the casino's edge.
3. that the player be sufficiently financed to exploit the bias.

Real versus Imaginary Bias

If we use 1,000 decisions as an example, how many times should a given number come up before we state that it is a real bias and not an imaginary one? In any study of *unbiased* wheels, in a thousand decisions, approximately half the numbers will be winners and half will be losers, and several numbers will come up a lot compared to their probability and some will come up relatively little. The following day, if we observe another 1,000 spins of that same *unbiased* wheel, we would see the same pattern — but with different numbers fluctuating between winners and losers. And so on with each 1,000 spins observed on this particular *unbiased* wheel. We'll see approximately half the numbers win, half lose, some come up a lot, some come up a little . . . and all the numbers would take turns being up and being down, until, after thousands of thousands of spins, we'd start to see the flattening out of probability as numbers started to settle into their long-range probabilities. This does not mean that the numbers will all be coming up exactly as probability predicts but the ratios will be close as the total number of decisions reaches into the hundreds of thousands and then millions.

That's on an *unbiased* wheel.

On a *biased* wheel, you would notice almost the exact same pattern with two big exceptions. You would note that a given number, or numbers, did not fluctuate between winning and losing (or losing very much). That as the total decisions increased, the truly biased number(s) would continue to win out of all proportion to its or their expectancy. You would see some fluctuations — up or down — but the overall performance would be up — way up in the case of a strongly biased number. If that "up" were able to overcome the casino's edge, then you would have a biased wheel you could win with. However, keep in mind that to win money at biased-wheel play, a number must come up more than once every 35 times, because the casino only pays 35 to one on a win. Numbers that come up more than once every 35 spins are the *golden* numbers and they are the key to the casino's treasury. Still even on unbiased wheels, after many thousands of spins, some numbers would have been winners and some numbers would have been losers, just by chance. It is the job of the wheel tracker to be able to distinguish, after thousands of spins, which numbers are coming up "at random" and which numbers are biased. The number one skill for the biased-wheel player is to be able to recognize the difference between a number that is just going through the normal fluctuations and a number that is truly *golden*. This is done by having a sufficiently large sample of decisions so that you can have confidence in your results.

The wheel tracker must also look for certain patterns. Often when one number is biased, it will rob hits from surrounding numbers. If there is glue in number **8**, then there's a good chance the numbers near **8** aren't going to get all that many hits because **8** has taken the play away from them. Or, if a given number is heavily biased, often other numbers near it are somewhat biased too. This is because the bias is in that portion of the wheel. This would be considered a biased section.

The key ingredient in discovering and exploiting biased wheels is having a sufficiently large sample of spins to make intelligent choices. How large is large enough?

According to John F. Julian in *The Julian Strategies in Roulette* (Paone Press), if you really want a high confidence rating (99%+) for your sampling then 3,800 decisions on a double-zero wheel and 3,700 decisions on a single-zero wheel would be the minimum amounts. You'll note that Julian has made it simple for those of us who hate math but want to use mathematical reasoning to help us achieve gambling success. By making the numbers correspond to 100 times the cycle (a cycle being 38 decisions with each number theoretically coming up once) we can say with confidence that each number would come up approximately 100 times . . . in theory. In practice, about half would come up more, and half would come up less. So then we ask ourselves, how much more would a number have to hit over its theoretical expectation in 3,800 or 3,700 spins for the wheel to be biased? Here many authors disagree. Being the conservative type, I prefer to go with the highest possible confidence rating. A single number would be biased (with a 99%+ chance of being right) on a double-zero wheel if it hit 140 times in 3800 spins. That's a one in 27 chance of occurring. It would be rare that this number of hits would be just random, given 3,800 spins. With such a biased wheel (one in 27), you would lose 26 bets and win one. For each winning bet, you would get odds of 35 to one. You'd be nine bets richer after every 27 spins (on average). On a single-zero wheel, you would have the same edge if the number hit 136 times out of 3,700 spins. This would be an extremely strong bias and one that could be exploited easily. The following chart will give various biased numbers based on Julian's recommended number of spins to give us the highest confidence rating. It will also show you what you would make if you bet the bias over a period of time. This is the *profit* per $100 wagered. This chart is for single-numbers only and

I've dropped all fractions (for simplicity). I'll cover groups of numbers and sections in a little while. However, realize that in any analysis of potentially biased wheels, if you note a strongly biased (A) number with two or three or four probably biased numbers hovering next to it, this could indicate a sector slice worth betting.

High Bias Confidence Group
3,800 Spins on Double-Zero Wheel and 3,700
Spins on Single-Zero Wheel

A= Strongly Biased; B = Biased; PB=Probably Biased; MB=Maybe Biased; R=Random

Total Hits	Approximate Ratio 00-Wheel	0-Wheel	Profit per $100 wagered 00-Wheel	0-Wheel	Rating
200	1 in 19	1 in 18	$47.22	$50.00	A
190	1 in 20	1 in 19	$44.44	$47.22	A
180	1 in 21	1 in 20	$41.67	$44.44	A
170	1 in 22	1 in 21	$38.89	$41.67	A
160	1 in 23	1 in 23	$36.11	$36.11	A
150	1 in 25	1 in 24	$30.56	$33.33	B
140	1 in 27	1 in 26	$25.00	$27.78	B
135	1 in 28	1 in 27	$22.22	$25.00	B
130	1 in 29	1 in 28	$19.44	$22.22	PB/B
125	1 in 30	1 in 29	$16.67	$19.44	PB
120	1 in 31*	1 in 30	$13.89*	$16.67	MB/PB
115	1 in 33*	1 in 32*	$ 8.33*	$11.11*	R
110	1 in 34*	1 in 33*	$ 5.56*	$ 8.33*	R
105	1 in 36*	1 in 35*	$ 0.00*	$ 2.78*	R

The starred* numbers indicate that the bias is not sufficient (or not really there) at 3,800 spins to warrant risking money. A number hitting 110 times or even 120 in 3,800 spins could just be the results of randomness. Add another 1,400 spins and if the bias still exists or has gotten stronger, then the number would be worth gambling on. You will probably never find a bias in the under 1 in 25 or 1 in 26 range. In addition, as you study 3,800 actual spins you will notice that even the strongest biased numbers will fluctuate up and down. Russell T. Barnhart, in *Beat the Wheel* (Carol Publishing), did an interesting study of an *artificially* biased wheel by counting the *0* and *00* as one number — *0/00*. This made the wheel a 37 pocket European model. The *0/00* was an artificially true bias that would appear on average once every 19 times — an extremely strong bias with a 100% confidence rating.

What he discovered was rather interesting. In 13 of the 14 days he clocked the artificially-biased wheel, the number *0/00* was either the number that hit the most or second most. That was to be expected. What was not expected was the fact that on day two, the *0/00* was the 18th highest number! Pure randomness had produced 17 numbers that hit with a greater frequency on one day than an incredibly strong biased number. Still, over the long haul, the biased number won out. The more spins you observe, the greater the accuracy of your readings.

How long would it take to clock a wheel for 3,800 or 3,700 spins? It's not that easy to figure. If the table is crowded, with many diverse bets, you might find that 30 decisions an hour is the most that can be expected. If the table is getting relatively little action, you could see 100 spins an hour (some authors estimate that you can see upwards of 120 to 140 spins per hour although I have never seen this). So, just for argument's sake, let's postulate an average of 65 decisions an hour. In 24 hours of play that would come to 1,560 decisions. It would take approximately 58 hours to clock 3,800 spins and approximately 57 hours to clock 3,700 spins. In other words, if you continuously clocked one wheel, you would know with high confidence whether it was biased or not at *the tenth hour of the third day*. That's a good name for a movie but a long time for one person to watch a wheel. That's why many of the great wheel trackers of history (all recounted in Barnhart's delightful book) worked in teams. Naturally, many people aren't interested in forming roulette teams on the speculation of finding strongly-biased wheels to play. If you fall into the lone wolf category but you still want to attempt biased wheel play, you could cut the sample size down by one-half (1,900/1,850 spins) or three-quarters (950/925 spins) and still have a decent chance of finding a true bias — if that bias were quite strong. Since you would want that bias to be have a better chance at being real than imagined, the shorter the run, the stronger the bias must be to bet good money on it. For fewer than 2,000 spins a one in 25 to a one in 29 ratio would be worth considering.

One wheel tracker I talked to had this to say: "I only clock 380 spins and I work on a base of 16. Any number that has come up 16 [1 in approximately 24] times, I'll bet on it for 190 spins. If it hasn't made me money in that time, I abandon the number. If a few numbers have hit this much, I'll bet all of them. I do one wheel a day, sometimes more if the casino has scoreboards."

This last is an important point. With the electronic scoreboards, a single player can clock several wheels at once, increasing the odds of finding a truly biased wheel. The flip side of that is the fact that the casinos can also clock their wheels (with much less effort than a player) by merely looking at the spreadsheet performance for any given wheel over a period of time. In this way, they can eliminate any strongly-biased wheels, especially if they discover that players have discovered the bias as well. Thus, like all technology, the electronic scoreboards have their good aspects and bad aspects. They make it easier for the wheel-tracker but they also make it easier for the casinos to stop the wheel tracker in his tracks (pun intended).

Biased Sectors

Often a sector of a wheel is biased, not just one number. Here's another wheel tracker's story: "At the [now-defunct] Sands in Las Vegas, I once played a strongly-biased wheel where the numbers 9 and 30 were hitting like crazy. Betting only one dollar to five dollars on the numbers 9, 26, 30 which is a three-sector slice on the double-zero wheel, I won $1,800 before the wheel was closed for inspection. I don't know what the management found but in a half day of playing I was hauling in the color [chips]. What was weird was that 26 didn't hit more than the expected frequency, maybe a little less in fact. Whatever was causing the bias, it was connected with 9 and

30 only. I was raking in the dough. Finally, the Sands management shut the wheel down. By that time I had won $1,800. The next day, the wheel was back in action but I didn't notice 'my' numbers hitting so I passed it by."

What kind of long-range study of a given wheel would give you a 99 percent confidence rating in a biased sector of two, three or four numbers? I would bet the entire sector of continuous numbers if in 1,900 spins those two, three or four numbers were each coming up more than 1 in 30. If we had each of five, six, seven or eight adjoining numbers coming up more than 1 in 31 times, I would take a shot at the entire sector.

Money Management on Biased Wheels

If you are playing a strongly-biased wheel with a high confidence rating, you will definitely win money — if you don't go broke first. While the foregoing sentence might sound ridiculous or bizarre, it is the truth. The mere fact that you are playing a strongly-biased wheel doesn't mean that on a given number of short-range decisions (say a half day's worth), you won't wind up losing. Check out Barnhart's experiment with the extremely-strong artificially-biased number. Had you been betting on the second day, you might have wound up a loser even though the number (0/00) was extremely biased. In the short run, luck and the odd bounce of the ball can even overcome a biased wheel. But in the long run, over thousands of spins, a strongly-biased wheel will win you money. The key is to have enough money behind you so that you can weather the fickleness of short-range fortune. Any money-management scheme for biased-wheel playing should take into account the strength of the bias. A strong bias doesn't need as much of a bankroll as a weak bias. A biased section doesn't need as much money as a single number. The following chart will give you some idea of the bankroll requirements necessary to play a biased-wheel or sector with a high degree of confidence so that you won't tap out and lose all your money.

Total Numbers Bet	Bias Type	Bet per spin	Total bankroll
1	1 in 30-33	one unit	3,000 units
1	1 in 27-29	one unit	2,600 units
1	1 in 24-26	one unit	2,000 units
1	1 in 20-25	one unit	1,800 units
2	1 in 30-33	two units	2,800 units
2	1 in 27-29	two units	2,400 units
2	1 in 24-26	two units	1,800 units
2	1 in 20-25	two units	1,600 units
3	1 in 30-33	three units	2,500 units
3	1 in 27-29	three units	2,100 units
3	1 in 24-26	three units	1,500 units
3	1 in 20-25	three units	1,300 units
4	1 in 30-33	four units	2,200 units
4	1 in 27-29	four units	1,800 units
4	1 in 24-26	four units	1,200 units
4	1 in 20-25	four units	1,000 units
5	1 in 30-33	five units	2,000 units
5	1 in 27-29	five units	1,600 units
5	1 in 24-26	five units	1,000 units
5	1 in 20-25	five units	850 units
6	1 in 30-33	six units	1,800 units
6	1 in 27-29	six units	1,400 units
6	1 in 24-26	six units	850 units
6	1 in 20-25	six units	650 units
7	1 in 30-33	seven units	1,700 units
7	1 in 27-29	seven units	1,300 units
7	1 in 24-26	seven units	750 units
7	1 in 20-25	seven units	550 units
8	1 in 30-33	eight units	1,600 units
8	1 in 27-29	eight units	1,200 units
8	1 in 24-26	eight units	650 units
8	1 in 20-25	eight units	450 units

A few common-sense observations are called for concerning any betting scheme. It is always better to have more money than less money behind you. That's a given. If you should start to see a serious decrease in your bankroll, reduce the size of your betting (if you are not already betting the table minimum) or temporarily abandon playing the wheel and record more hits to see if the bias returns. This last is an interesting phenomena, brilliantly analyzed in *The Biased Wheel Handbook* by Mark Billings and Brent Fredrickson (Saros Designs Publishing). Some biases are extremely strong over several thousand spins and then suddenly vanish for several thousands of spins and then, just as suddenly, they return. Billings and Fredrickson have come up with an ingenious explanation for this effect which has been noted but never sufficiently analyzed by other biased-wheel researchers. So keep in mind, if you have been playing and winning at a biased wheel and then that bias seems to vanish, it just might return. Stop playing and record. When you have recorded a sufficient number of spins to ascertain whether the bias is gone for good or just gone temporarily, then you make your decision to play or run away from that particular wheel. [A good question here is — how do you know when to stop playing a wheel that has been biased? I mean, the wheel doesn't suddenly call out to you: "Hey, Mac, I'm not biased right now!" You have to use some rule of thumb to tell you this information. My rule of thumb would be to stop playing and record another 380 hits if I haven't won money in the past 200 spins.]

The difference between a money-management scheme on a biased wheel and a money-management scheme for other types of play is the difference between night and day. When you play blackjack or craps, or any other table game including layout strategies in roulette, you generally have a predetermined session in mind: how many hours, how much money won or lost, and so forth, before you call it a session or a day. Not so when you are playing a biased wheel. Once you have determined with a sufficient degree of confidence that you are actually playing at a biased wheel, then you want to play it and play it and play it. If you have a willing spouse, or friend, or teammate, you would want to play the wheel around the clock if you could. Why? Because once the casino gets an idea that the wheel is biased, the casino will shut it down.

Naturally, there are ways to cover your biased-wheel betting in order to prevent the precipitate closing of a table. You could make some even money bets. For example, if you have several biased numbers and the majority of them are red, then bet a small bet on red. If, through happenstance, the majority of your numbers tend to fit into the arbitrary Dozens or Columns arrangements on the layout, then place a bet in these, too. This is called masking your play. Another good scheme is to check out the numbers that have been winning closest to your biased number and place small bets on these. This phenomenon, which I have dubbed the halo effect, will often see numbers near biased numbers hitting with a greater (or lesser) frequency. Do not, however, simply bet at random on the other numbers. The house has a terrific edge and unless your bias is very strong indeed, you might find yourself getting hammered by trying a masking technique that eats up too much of your bankroll. Still, masking one's play, when done properly, can give you extra winning hours at the table.

Another thing you don't want to do is call attention from other players to yourself. The pit is going to notice you; after all, that's their job. But you don't want other players picking up on what you're doing. So don't make a big deal of your wins. Exchange the roulette chips for regular casino chips occasionally, so that it doesn't look to the other players that you are making a killing. Put the regular chips in your pocket. This will prevent "mimics" from betting with you — this is Chameleon betting, a great technique, that I discuss in Chapter Eight.

Biased-wheel play is the single best method for winning money at roulette. The more spins you clock, the greater the confidence in your bias. For the purposes of our discussion, it isn't necessary to know what exactly causes wheels to become biased. In fact, on a given wheel, even with a bias of monumental proportions, you will probably never know what caused it. But you will know how to play it. And you will win. For the gambler that is all that is important.

If this chapter has whetted your appetite to really pursue biased-wheel play, then I strongly recommend that you read and study *The Biased Wheel Handbook* by Mark Billings and Brent Fredrickson. Although the price of this spiral-bound book is rather steep — $79.95 — it is worth the money if biased-wheel play has hit a responsive cord in you and you want to become a professional or semiprofessional wheel tracker. I will have more to say about this book and some other recommended roulette books in Chapter Twelve.

However, for most players, clocking wheels (even a smallish 380 spins) requires too much time and effort. Most roulette players do not go to a casino frequently enough to put in the amount of time required to catch a biased wheel. If you are visiting a casino for two or even three days, you aren't going to want to spend them clocking wheels and not playing. "Hooray, I found a biased wheel but then I had to go home!" just doesn't have the ring of truth about it. Still many roulette players want some short-term methods to exploit *possibly* biased wheels. If you are going to play roulette in a casino for a day or several days, it can't hurt to attempt to position yourself to take advantage of possibly biased wheels. These short-term methods of exploiting possibly biased wheels are the subject of the chapters coming up.

6

The Double Dynamite Roulette System:

BIG Number and Sector Slicing

The safest and best way to spin roulette gold is to play a biased wheel with a strong degree of confidence. Not everyone wants to spend the time and effort necessary to do that. Still, there is a way to have your cake and eat it too — to coin a kaon — by applying short-term strategies that might, just might, be exploiting strongly biased or temporarily biased wheels. If 3,800 spins of a roulette wheel seem daunting, certainly 16 or 20 recorded decisions would be easy to handle — especially if those 16 to 20 decisions were already recorded for you.

I call this method of play *the Double Dynamite Roulette System* because you are combining the two best long-term methods of play, BIG (or Golden) Number play and Sector Slicing, as short-term methods of play into your arsenal. It's just a question of keeping track of 16 to 20 spins before you engage in any betting.

Enter the casinos to our rescue. Whenever possible, we'll use the casinos' scoreboards to do the work for us. These scoreboards record the last 16 or 20 numbers that have hit. Just make a note of these numbers and look for the following:

1. Are an inordinate number of hits (say, eight to 12) in a given one-third, one-quarter, or one-eighth section of the wheel? If so, bet that section. This is a sector slice.

2. Have certain numbers repeated, even though the overall hits have been scattered? If so, bet those numbers. These are BIG Numbers.

3. Are certain numbers repeating within a sector of the wheel where other numbers have also hit? Then bet those numbers and the other numbers in that sector — even if some of the numbers in that sector haven't hit.

The only question you have to ask yourself is how much money should you wager on any given spin. My advice is to play conservatively — but that's *always* my advice. Remember, the fact that you are perceiving a pattern doesn't mean that the pattern is truly caused by a biased wheel. Caution is advised when risking one's money.

If the sector is eight to 12 numbers, one unit on each number would be sufficient. Give yourself 200 units to play. If you lose those 200 units, move on. A unit is *your* minimum bet, not necessarily the table minimum. For example, if the table minimum is $10, spread that $10 out over 12 numbers using one-dollar units on each (this will, of course, come to $12). If the sector is five numbers, spread that $10 out in two-dollar unit bets.

Using the Double Dynamite Roulette strategy is not a guarantee that you will be playing a biased wheel. Indeed, most times you won't. However, so what? Inside bettors will be facing that 5.26 (or 2.70) percent edge no matter what system they choose to employ. Why not at least have a shot at taking advantage of *potentially* biased wheels? There is no downside to the Double Dynamite Roulette System. If the wheel isn't biased, you haven't increased your chances of losing. But if the wheel is biased (for whatever reason), then you have definitely increased your chances of winning, perhaps markedly so if that bias is strong and long-term. For roulette players interested in the short-run pleasures of the game and the possibility of making off with some money, it really doesn't get much better than that.

Apropos of this, a wonderful new roulette card for short-term play has hit the market, developed by Joe Zanghi who has his "tip tricks" in Chapter Seven. The product is called

Roulette Action Play Tracker Card. It's a plastic card that has all the numbers of the roulette wheel facing you in a readable fashion. The *0* is at the top, the *00* at the bottom. Mr. Zanghi has also created a single-zero roulette tracker card for those fortunate enough to play this roulette wheel. The tracker card can only be used for short-run play as five or six dots are all you can fit in any given spoke. You use a water-based marker to record the hits as dots. This gives you an easily readable wheel. You'll be able to note quickly if you're dealing with sectors, BIG Numbers or a combination of both. When you're finished with your play, you can erase the card and reuse it next time.

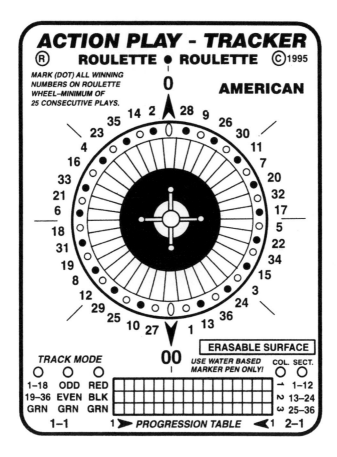

Figure Four:
Action Play Roulette Tracker Card
American Double-Zero Wheel

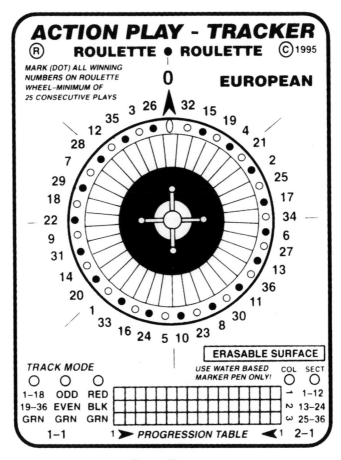

Figure Five:
Action Play Roulette Tracker Card
European Single-Zero Wheel

Although Zanghi's playing advice is a little more aggressive than mine, his "Tracker" system is a good investment ($6.95) since the card is reusable. I used it to clock wheels (short-term only) for 29 straight days in Las Vegas in the summer of 1996 and it served me well.

In all cases, we will assume that the table minimum bet is $10 and that you will spread this $10 around in units of one, two, three or more depending on the type of short-term pattern you're attempting to exploit. Your unit bet will be considered one dollar. Thus, we are giving ourselves $200 to play any of these scoreboards — which is a generous amount for short-term play on a given wheel.

I think what you'll discover is that short-term "biased-wheel play" strategies can be fun and challenging but not daunting. Such play is probably the only way to have a shot at taking home the money in this game without becoming a wheel-tracking pro.

On the following pages, I will show you diagrams of various roulette patterns based on real wheels and their scoreboards. Then in the paragraph accompanying these diagrams, I'll discuss various ways to play the short-term patterns that have appeared. Most of the scoreboards recorded 20 numbers, although some recorded 16. All the hits were recorded on the *Action Play Roulette Tracker* card developed by Joe Zanghi. You will note that on the diagrams the outer ring contains the numbers, next to the numbers is a black dot or an open "o." The black dot means the number is black. The "o" means the number is red. The large "0" means it's green. To record numbers you simply place a dot inside the spoke portion corresponding to that number. That's all there is to the mechanics of recording the hits.

Although the concept behind the Double Dynamite Roulette System is to find biased wheels (and perhaps section-shooting dealers if they exist — see Chapter Seven), the fact that we are only looking at 16 or 20 recorded hits does not give us any certainty or confidence in our judgments. True biased-wheel play would require several thousand decisions as discussed in the previous chapter.

Still, short of blind luck, attempting to use long-range playing strategies such as the BIG Number method and the Sector Slicing method for short-term play cannot hurt us. If a roulette wheel is strongly biased, you have an excellent shot at winning because you are going to be playing the numbers or sections that are hitting. This is far better for the short-term player than playing the numbers or sectors that *aren't* hitting in the hopes that these numbers and sectors will catch up.

How to Judge a BIG Number

In short-term play, we are going to judge BIG numbers as follows:

1. Four or more hits out of 20 = very strong BIG Number.
2. Three or more hits out of 16 = very strong BIG Number.
3. Three hits out of 20 = strong BIG Number.
4. Two hits out of 16 = moderate BIG Number.
5. Two hits out of 20 = weak BIG Number.

How to Judge a Sector Slice

For sector slicing, we will consider the following criteria as the basis of betting a given sector:

1. If no number has hit more than once (an unusual occurrence), then any sector that has six or more adjacent numbers that have hit, we will play all those numbers.
2. If two sectors have an equal number of hits but one sector has one or more BIG Numbers, we will play the sector that has the BIG Numbers.
3. The minimum adjacent numbers to be considered a sector is three, if one or two of the three is/are BIG Number(s).
4. If there seems to be a sector with BIG Numbers and a gap where one number has not hit, we will bet that sector, including the number that did not hit.
5. All BIG Numbers are bet, but not all sectors are bet. When in doubt, BIG Numbers take precedence over sectors.

Money Management Using the Double Dynamite System

As stated, we are going to assume that the table minimum is $10. This is a reasonable table minimum that will be found in many casinos, especially on the weekends. We are also going to assume that you can bet this $10 minimum in units of one dollar. Thus, one dollar is our minimum betting unit.

If we were playing a BIG Number or Sector Slice of numbers with a high confidence rating — having done the necessary clocking of the wheel for hundreds or thousands of spins — then we would not be deterred by short-term losses and we would play until the cows came home, the chickens came home to roost, the swallows returned . . . well, you get the picture. However, our play must be dictated, as previously stated, by caution. Give yourself no more than $200 dollars at a given BIG Number wheel before moving to another wheel. If you are betting a sector of eight to 12 numbers (which won't happen very often) give yourself no more than $100 or 10 spins. That amount will give you a healthy whack at your BIG Numbers and sectors — 10 or 20 spins. If you aren't ahead after this, move on. If you are ahead, go for another 10 or 20 spins. Keep playing until the 10 or 20 spins results in a loss. Then move on.

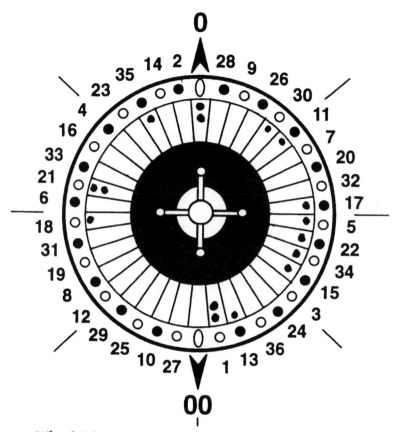

Wheel # 1:

Scoreboard: 16 numbers recorded. This diagram shows three moderate BIG Numbers — *0*, 21, 1 — which have hit twice each and a five number section — **17,** 5, **22,** 34, **15.** Take your $10 minimum bet and spread it out as on all eight numbers. You'll have two dollars left over. Put this on *0* and 1 as *0* and 1 are closest to the sector that has hit. Note also that of 16 hits, 11 have occurred on one half of the wheel between *0* and 1.

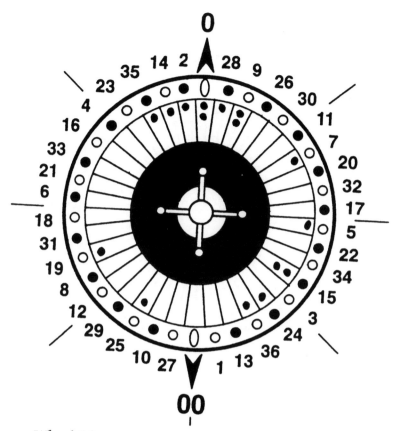

Wheel # 2:

Scoreboard: 16 numbers recorded. This diagram shows three moderate BIG numbers which have hit twice — *0, 9,* **15** — two of which (*0* and 9) are also in a sector slice of six numbers — **35,** 14, **2,** *0,* **28,** 9. Take your $10 minimum bet and spread it as follows. Put two dollars on each of the BIG Numbers (*0,* 9, **15**) and one dollar on each number in the sector slice (**35,** 14, **2, 28**).

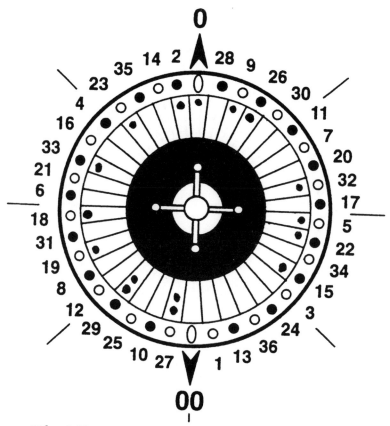

Wheel #3:

Scoreboard: 16 numbers recorded. This diagram shows two moderate BIG Numbers (27 and **29**) but no sector of more than two hits (although two sectors 32 through **15** and **2** through **26** only have two and one gaps between numbers respectively). Either bet five dollars on each of the two BIG Numbers or pass this wheel by.

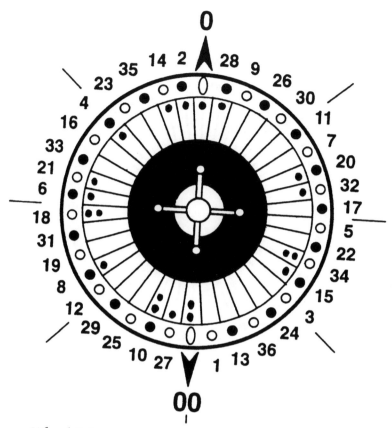

Wheel # 4:

Scoreboard: 20 numbers recorded. This diagram shows four weak BIG Numbers (**10**, *00*, 18, 34) and one weak four-number slice (14, **2**, *0*, **28**). Two of the four BIG Numbers (**10** and *00*) are one number apart, a number that has also hit (27). Bet two dollars on each BIG number and two dollars on number 27.

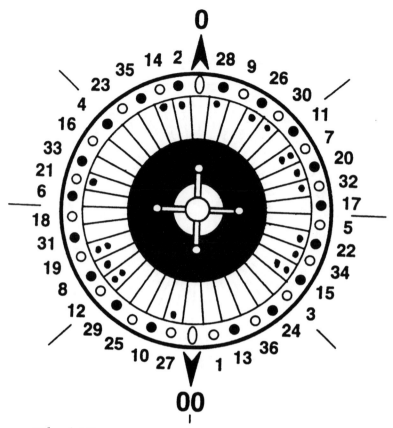

Wheel # 5:

Scoreboard: 20 numbers recorded. This diagram shows four weak BIG Numbers that have each hit twice (19, 12, 7, **15**). Each BIG Number is a part of three-number slices, with 19 and 12 in one such slice. Bet two dollars on each BIG Number and two dollars on number **8**, which is the number between 19 and 12.

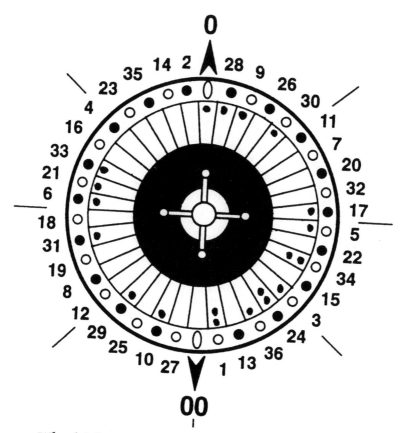

Wheel # 6:

Scoreboard: 20 numbers recorded. This diagram shows three weak BIG Numbers that have hit twice each (34, **24,** 1) all within a seven numbered slice (1 through 34). Two other numbers in this slice have also hit (36 and 3). Bet two dollars on each BIG Number and one dollar on **13,** 36, 3 and **15.**

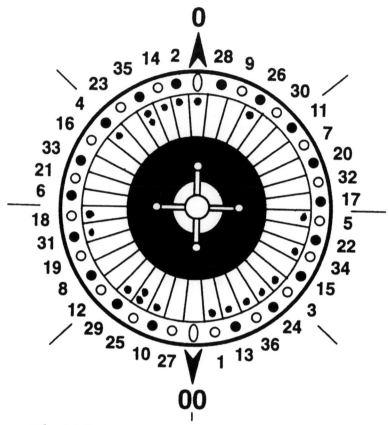

Wheel # 7:

Scoreboard: 20 numbers recorded. This diagram shows two weak BIG Numbers (**35** and 25) and three slices: one composed of five numbers (1, **13,** 36, **24,** 3), one composed of four numbers (**35,** 14, **2,** *0*) and one composed of three numbers (**29,** 25, **10**). Bet either five dollars on each BIG Number or one dollar on each number in the three slices ($12 total).

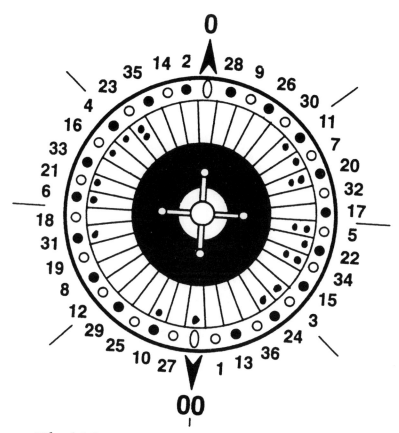

Wheel # 8:

Scoreboard: 20 numbers recorded. This diagram shows four weak BIG Numbers that have each hit twice (23, **20**, 5, 34) with three of them hitting relatively close together (**20,** 5, 34). Bet two dollars on each of the BIG Numbers and two dollars on **22.**

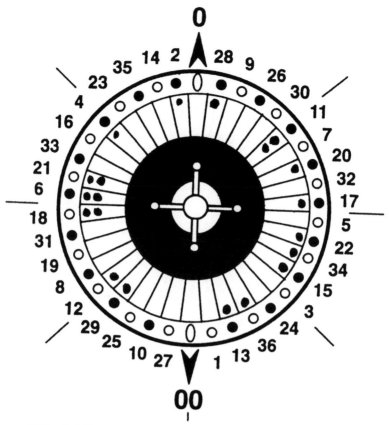

Wheel # 9:

Scoreboard: 20 numbers recorded. This diagram shows four weak BIG Numbers that have each hit twice (21, **6**, 18, **11**), the first three of which are next to each other. Bet three dollars each on 21, **6** and 18 and two dollars on **11**. (Total wager is $11.)

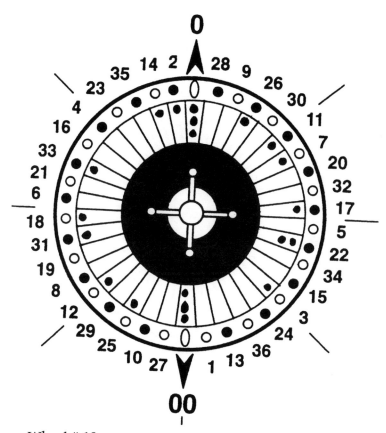

Wheel # 10:

Scoreboard: 20 numbers recorded. This diagram shows two strong BIG Numbers that have hit three times each (*0* and *00*) that are on opposite sides of the wheel. It also has one weak BIG Number that has hit twice (**22**). Bet four dollars on *0* and *00*; and two dollars on **22**.

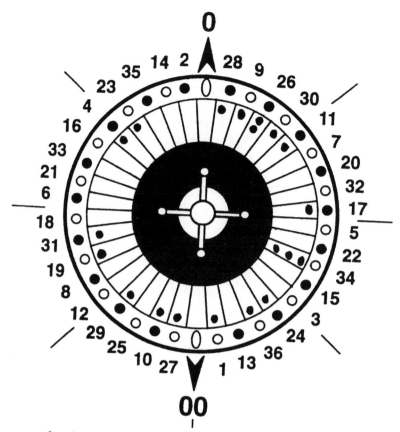

Wheel # 11:

Scoreboard: 20 numbers recorded. This diagram shows one strong BIG number (34) that hit three times and one weak BIG Number that hit twice (26) which is in the middle of five numbers that hit (28, 9, 26, 30, 11). Bet four dollars on 34 and two dollars on 26. Bet one dollar on 28, 9, 30 and 11.

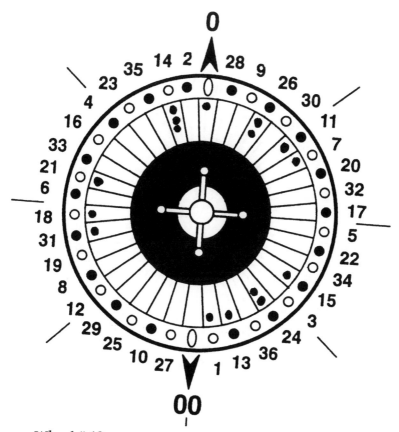

Wheel # 12:

Scoreboard: 16 numbers recorded. This diagram shows one very strong BIG Number that hit three times (14) and two moderate BIG Numbers that each hit twice (**24** and **26**). Bet six dollars on 14 and two dollars on **24** and **26**. In this diagram there are no sectors to even consider.

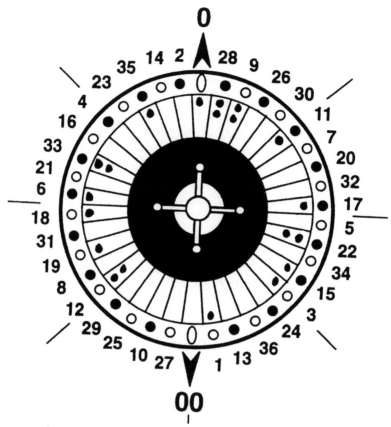

Wheel # 13:

Scoreboard: 20 numbers recorded. This diagram shows five weak BIG Numbers that have each hit twice (**28,** 9 — next to each other — **22,** 12, **33**). Bet two dollars on each of these numbers. You also might want to bet one dollar on the *0,* which forms a three number sector with **28** and 9.

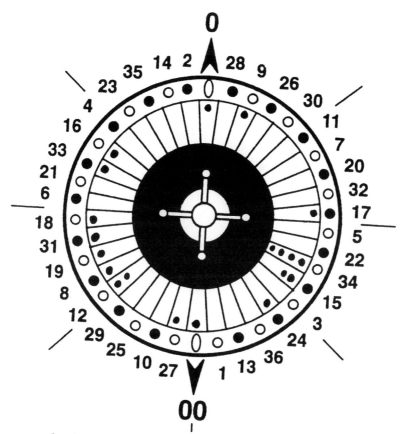

Wheel # 14:

Scoreboard: 20 numbers recorded. This diagram shows two weak BIG Numbers that have each hit twice (**15** and 12) and one very strong BIG Number that has hit four times (34). Note that 34 is next to **15**. Also note that 12 is the tail end of a sector slice of five hits. Bet four dollars on 34 and one dollar on **15,** 12, **8,** 19, **31** and 18.

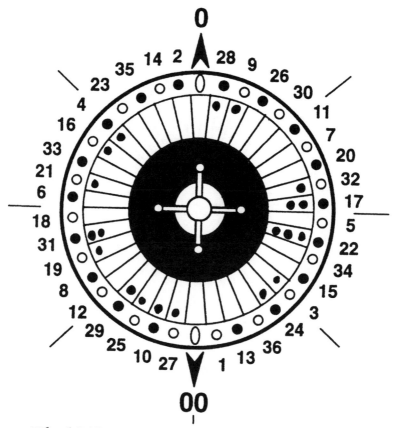

Wheel # 15:

Scoreboard: 20 numbers recorded. This diagram shows one strong BIG Number (**22**) and two weak BIG Numbers (**17** and **31**). However, **17** is only one number removed from **22**. This also shows a four number slice (**29**, 25, **10**, 27). Bet one dollar on 32, two dollars on **17**, one dollar on 5, four dollars on **22** and two dollars on **31**. You are betting one dollar on 5 since it is in the center of a number of hits.

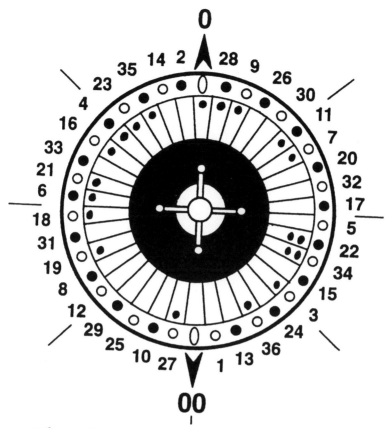

Wheel # 16:

Scoreboard: 20 numbers recorded. This diagram shows two weak BIG Numbers (**22** and 34) but they are side by side on the wheel. It also shows seven hits in an eight-number sector (18, **6,** 21, 16, **4,** 23, **35**). Bet one dollar on all the numbers in the sector, including **33** which didn't hit, and one dollar each on **22** and 34.

7

The Unicorns of Roulette:

Sector Shooting and Dealer Signatures

One of the most controversial areas of roulette study concerns whether some dealers have the ability to control where the ball will land. If the dealer can aim the ball at a given section of the wheel and hit it with a greater-than-average frequency, that dealer can change the game from a random one with a predetermined house edge, to a game that either increases or decreases the house's edge, or gives the edge to the player. A dealer who can consciously hit a predetermined section of the wheel is called a section shooter. On the other hand, another argument is made for dealers having an *unconscious* ability or trait to place the ball, not so much in a given section, but a given distance from the last hit. This unconscious ability or trait is called *dealer signing* or a *dealer signature*. These are the unicorns of roulette and experts have lined up on both sides of each issue. Some say they are myths, some say they are real talents. So, let's take a look at the arguments for and against each "talent" and see whether either or both can be taken advantage of by the player.

Section Shooting

Argument For:

Mr. Rousseau has dealt roulette for years. And spin after spin, day after day, for weeks, months, years, he has practiced controlling the ball and understanding speed. Now, he can, just by looking at the speed of the rotor, judge what kind of force is necessary to propel the ball in such a way that after many revolutions around the track, it will fall into a predetermined one-quarter or one third of the wheel. In fact, so good is he at timing everything, that he has even figured how to take advantage of the barriers that cause the ball to drop inconsistently — as opposed to a smooth arc — into the pockets. Of course, he is not perfect, what man or woman is? He is only accurate 50 percent of the time. Still, this means that he is quite consistent. Half the time he spins that ball, it will land in the quarter or third that he has selected. Roulette for him, and for anyone who plays at his table, is no longer random, it is predictable and controlled to a great extent. Mr. Rousseau's talent can be used to help a player or help the house. He decides which.

Impossible? No. This is a physical talent that Mr. Rousseau has, not some supernatural ability. It's eye and hand coordination. Judgment. Like walking a tightrope or being an Olympic gymnast or a surgeon. Not everyone can do it. But not everyone can fly on a trapeze, either, or throw a curve ball. But that doesn't mean a select few, the professionals, can't do it. And how hard is it to judge speed, acceleration, deceleration, and future positioning, anyway? Anyone who drives a car does this sort of thing every day. As you enter a highway, you have to judge the speed of the oncoming cars, their distance, your speed, how your acceleration will affect the distance of the them-to-you ratio. You have to accurately gauge all this in order to merge with traffic on any highway in America. A relative piece of cake. I mean, little old ladies do it. (Okay, okay, little old men, too.) Thus, any dealer that puts in the time to learn how to control the fall of the ball, will probably be able to do it. It is a physical ability like anything else. It may be a little harder than driving a car, but with practice,

it can be done. What would it take? Simply to know and exe-
cute a spin of so many revolutions starting from a predetermined moment — say when *00* was at your hand. Zap! you let
the ball go, it spins so many revolutions, falls just so, and hits
the section you want it to hit.

Witnesses For:

No less an authority than Laurance Scott, author of *How
to Beat Roulette* (Dona Ana, $295 with video) and the advocate
and teacher of a method of visually tracking the ball and
where it will fall, stated in the June 1991 issue of *Blackjack
Forum* that some dealers actually do have the ability to sector
shoot and that many casinos use such dealers to cheat the
players. In another issue of *Blackjack Forum* (March 1992) a pit
boss from Atlantic City wrote the following: "Section shooting
is not a myth. This was proven to me in a proficient demonstration by a person who had dealt the game of roulette for
more than two decades. This person was many years my se-
nior and my teacher. Section shooting is a common, sought-
after skill in the realm of roulette dealers. For this reason,
dealers who are supervised in professional gambling casinos
are not permitted to hawk stares into the roulette wheel." Joe
Zanghi, the developer of the *Action Play Roulette* Tracker card,
has given the game of roulette a lot of thought. He even has
his own roulette wheel. He is a passionate spokesman for
wheel tracking — perhaps the only method of beating roulette
in the long run — but he also believes that many dealers can
and do control where the ball will fall. "No dealer can control
the exact pocket where a ball will fall, but a one-third to one-
half section of the wheel is well within certain dealers' abili-
ties." In his book, *The Julian Strategies in Roulette*, John F. Julian
wrote that he had interviewed several dealers who claimed
that they could "locate" the ball. Unfortunately, Julian didn't
ask for a demonstration. Finally, one editor of a gaming magazine that is now defunct, told me that he personally knew of
a team of cheats working Atlantic City who were in league
with section-shooting dealers. "It's easy, the team bets on
those numbers that the other players aren't betting on — in a
given sector of eight to 12 numbers. Some of the numbers

overlap with other players but many do not. This way, the table doesn't lose money even though the cheats are winning. At the end of the cheating dealer's day, the roulette wheel looks statistically much like any other wheel. In fact, it isn't. The cheats have made off with a bundle that they share with the dealers." This editor claimed he had personally talked to the individuals involved in this.

Argument Against:

The roulette wheel does not spin at a constant speed. It is not a perpetual-motion machine and thus it slows with each revolution. At a certain point in the game, it must be respun. Most casinos have their dealers spin the ball in the opposite direction of the wheel's spin (some casinos have the dealers mix it up). With the numbers rushing up at the dealer in a blur how could the dealer's small motor coordination be so perfect as to release the ball within a breath's difference each time as to have it land in a given section — even a given one-half of the wheel? Add to this that the dealer has other duties, like watching the game, sizing bets and payoffs, and you wonder what good would it do the honest dealer to try to develop such a talent if such a talent could be developed. The fact is that the barriers on the track, the wind in the casino, the humidity, the change in the spin rate of the wheel, the size of the ball, the smoke in the air, all conspire to make accurate placing or even inaccurate placing (but winning placing) an impossible dream. Despite the fact that it is a physical ability, it is one that cannot be developed. It would not be like tightrope walking but tightrope walking on a line as thin as fishing tackle in a heavy wind! It might be theoretically possible that someone, somewhere, sometime could do it, still even the best tightrope walkers in the world today would fail time and again to get across. The line is just too thin; the wind just too strong. Thus, the precision needed to place the ball is just *too* precise and the margin for error is just too big. Even a split heartbeat's delay in releasing the ball would create an enormous difference in which numbers were passing the ball at that moment and where that ball would eventually end up. The sector-shooting dealer is attempting to predict a chaotic situation that has too many variables — it is tantamount to attempting to predict what effects a butterfly's flapping of its wings will have on the hurricane strength in the Gulf. Can't be done.

Witnesses Against:

In the December 1992 issue of *Blackjack Forum*, publisher Arnold Snyder conducted an interview with Paul Tramble, Sr., owner and founder of Paul Tramble Roulette Services, Inc. of Reno, Nevada. Mr. Tramble has a wide knowledge of roulette as it is not only his business but his passion. He stated in no uncertain terms that too much was required of a dealer to be able to section shoot with accuracy. In the same issue both Steve Forte, an expert in gaming and cheating techniques, and Bill Eadington, head of the economics department at The University of Nevada and the coordinator of the International Gambling Conference, weighed in on the negative side of the section-shooting debate. Eadington stated that in his entire career he had never seen a demonstration of this ability nor had he ever heard about any dealer in Nevada with the talent. Forte stated: "Finally, the most obvious factor, and remarkably, the one that many seem to forget: section shooting is the act of correlating perfectly two questionably attainable skills, not one. The dealer has to aim twice! He must first push the rotor to a predetermined speed, and then spin the ball with a predetermined force. The actions must be executed naturally and without suspicion. Compare these actions with those of professional bowlers, golfers, pool players and similar athletes. These pros can only aim once and can literally take as much time as they want to warm up, evaluate and calculate their actions." Finally, Darwin Ortiz, author of two excellent books on casino gaming — *Darwin Ortiz on Casino Gambling* and *Gambling Scams* (both from Carol Publishing) — has also come down squarely against the idea that some dealers can control the ball's ultimate destination.

My Research:

I spoke to many dealers in Atlantic City, the Midwest and Las Vegas concerning the possibility of sector shooting. Here's

what I found: Surprisingly, most of the dealers had no idea
what I was referring to when I said "sector shooting." This is
particularly true of the younger dealers. It seems that they are
unaware of the lore surrounding roulette and their only interest in the game seems to be dealing it correctly (as it should be,
I guess). Not one of the younger dealers had read even a single book on roulette, and only two of 20 had read any book on
gambling at all! When I explained what I meant by sector
shooting, they uniformly agreed that they were too busy dealing the game to bother with trying to locate the ball in a given
pocket or sector. "It would give me a headache watching the
wheel spin," said one young female dealer. "I never thought
about it," said a young male dealer. "But maybe I could do it
if I tried hard enough. Although it seems like a waste of time."
The younger dealers were split as to whether someone could
do it with practice. All agreed that they wouldn't want to
bother and most felt that if they tried, they would probably
fail as it would be a skill that was beyond their capability.

Most of the middle-aged and older dealers had heard of
the concept. Most of them rejected it, saying it was an impos-
sibility. A few dealers said that they thought it was possible
and one dealer said he thought some dealers in the "old days"
could do it. None of the dealers I spoke to said that they could
do it.

Still, the fact that some people, many people, most people,
or almost all people on earth can't do a certain thing doesn't
mean it can't be done by many other people, some other people, or a few other people. That is essentially John F. Julian's
argument. There might be sector-shooting dealers out there;
there might not be sector-shooting dealers out there. If there
are, by playing BIG Number and sector-slice roulette, you
might stumble upon them and be able to exploit them. Of
course, if a dealer were cheating for the house, as Laurance
Scott maintains, you would find that your BIG Numbers suddenly deflated and your sectors disappeared when the dealer
saw where you were placing your bets.

If you were convinced that a dealer was deliberately spinning the ball to make you lose, then you would have a choice.
You could wait until he spins before placing your bets (probably betting on numbers that haven't been covered based on

the assumption that these are the ones he's shooting for) or you can leave the table. I'd leave.

There is a third option. Get the dealer to shoot for your numbers.

How to Tip the Dealer to Tip the Game in Your Favor!

Joe Zanghi, who thinks dealers might be able to control the ball, has hit upon a method to exploit just such possible dealer sector shooting. It's worth a look. If you study the typical American wheel, you will notice that if you place the *0* at the top and the *00* at the bottom, the numbers **17** and 18 are on opposite sides of the wheel and both are approximately halfway between the *0* and *00*. Zanghi's idea is to place a small tip on either **17** or 18 and let the dealer know about it. He feels that because either number is equidistant between the *0* and *00*, it is an inviting target for the dealers to shoot for. The *0* and *00* are easy markers. Once you've placed the tip, you bet the **17** or 18 and you also bet the three or four numbers on either side of it. That gives you seven or nine numbers working and a dealer who might just be ready, willing and able to hit those numbers as he aims for **17** or 18. Using Zanghi's idea can't hurt and it could help, especially if the dealer has been hitting those sections containing either the **17** or 18. If you find that after three or four tipping attempts the dealer isn't able to hit the sector slice that you're betting, then you might have to abandon that wheel and seek a new table.

Dealer Signatures

Dealers get into a rhythm. They pick up the ball from the pocket where it last hit the same way each time. They then spin it the same way each time, with the same force. Thus, the ball will spin the same number of spins and should land the same *number of pockets* away from the last spin. This *unconscious* ability or trait to place the ball, not so much in a given section, but a given distance from the last hit is called *dealer signing* or a *dealer signature.* Again, experts have lined up on either side of the dealer signature issue with the same results. Essentially, it boils down to a matter of belief. Some experts believe that some dealers unconsciously do this; some experts believe there is no consistency to the distance that the ball travels from one spin to the next and, with the changing rotor spin over time, it would be impossible to achieve consistency anyway. Essentially, the arguments are the same as for the conscious ability to sector shoot.

However, the dealer signature is an interesting concept and I tend to give it some credence because — one, it makes sense, and two, I *want* to believe it's true. Of course, if one could follow a thousand dealers and record their spins over thousands of decisions, it might be possible to determine once and for all whether the signature idea is a myth or a reality. To this date, I know of no such extensive study as this. The actual accomplishing of such a study would be much more difficult than just the recording of thousands of dealers and thousands of their spins. Since we are looking for an *unconscious* ability that these dealers might have, we wouldn't want them to know that we are studying them because that would affect their spins. Once dealers realized that we were looking at them specifically, they would become highly conscious of what they were doing. If any signature actually existed with such a dealer, their awareness of their spinning technique would very quickly erase whatever signature they had. So the study of possible signatures would have to be done surreptitiously, without the dealer noticing, and there's the rub. How could a researcher stand by a dealer's table, follow the dealer from table to table, hour after hour, day after day, recording and analyzing his spins without the dealer becoming aware of such a person? At first the dealer might think that the wheel was being clocked, but it wouldn't take long for him to suspect that it was *his spins* that were being clocked. Even if the dealer didn't think it was he but the machine being clocked, this might cause him to alter his spin.

Now, wouldn't a biased-wheel watcher also affect a dealer's spin? Yes. Certainly a dealer would eventually become aware of someone standing near his table recording thousands of spins to ascertain whether the wheel was biased.

Yes, it might make the dealer self-conscious. Yes, the dealer might change how he spins the ball. But, in truth, none of this would matter. On a biased wheel any number of dealers will spin the ball with any amount of force, causing the ball to make any number of revolutions around the wheel, and all this wouldn't affect the bias one whit because that bias was in the wheel itself and had nothing to do with the spinning of the ball or the dealer. But anything that is dealer-dependent and dependent on the dealer being unaware is immediately changed when the dealer becomes aware. In this case, as in quantum mechanics in physics, the observer interferes with the observed by the mere fact that he is observing! And good-bye dealer signature. So I doubt if an actual practical test of dealer signatures is workable in the real world of casino play.

The other way to look at it is that dealer signatures must necessarily vary as the wheel speed slows down over time. The dealer might spin the ball the same way time and again but with each ball-spin he is playing into a fractionally different wheel-spin. Thus, dealer signatures would move slowly around the wheel as the wheel itself slowed. When the wheel was respun and thus accelerated, you would see the same patterns as last time. You would have to then analyze the pattern of the signature — an even more complicated task.

Still, if dealer signatures exist, certainly they would be exploitable in long- and short-term play, especially short-term play as the gradual slowing of the wheel's spin would not affect the signature quite so drastically. As I see it, we have a situation very much like the situation we saw in the last chapter where we used BIG Number and Sector Slicing as short-term playing strategies in the hope — as opposed to the expectation — that we were playing biased wheels. So let us now use the dealer signature concept the same way. If the dealer signature exists, then it will help us to win. If it doesn't exist, it can't hurt us — since it isn't increasing the odds against us. We merely face the same awful odds we would have faced had we played any layout strategy. Still, analyzing signatures is a technique of play that might be able to change the odds in our favor. It's worth a try.

Finding Possible Signatures

In any series of decisions, it is easy to find the "average" distance of a dealer's spins from decision to decision. Just add up the distance of each spin and divide by the total number of spins. Unfortunately, this is not the same as finding a signature. What we want to know is if the dealer's average is within the confines of, say, one-third of the wheel. That is to say, will the dealer spin the ball in such a way that it tends to land within a nine to 12 pocket grouping consistently?

Looking at the double-zero roulette wheel, let us say that on spin number one the dealer picks the ball up from the 00 pocket and spins it so that it winds up in the 12 pocket, five pockets away. On his next spin, he picks the ball up from the 12 pocket and spins it so that it lands in the 6 pocket, five pockets away from the 12. Finally on this third spin, he lands it in the 23 pocket — another five pockets away. The dealer's signature here would be five. Of course, three spins of the wheel is not enough to determine without a doubt that a dealer has a signature, but for purposes of a glaring example it is sufficient. Since the last number that hit was 23, we would now bet on 9 — five pockets away. In the best of all possible worlds, the dealer would again spin the ball in such a way that it would land in our 9 — five pockets away.

In the real world, as opposed to the world of my roulette dreams, we would never see a perfect signature. What we would want to find is a dealer who places the ball more than a third of the time within a 12 pocket grouping an average distance away. Let us say that the dealer is able to hit a 12 number grouping, one half of the time. In this way, we would bet those 12 numbers (12 units), lose half the time (-12 units) and win half the time because one of our 12 numbers hit; this means we lose 11 units on the numbers that didn't hit but win 35 units on the number that did hit for a net win of 24 units (35-11 = 24). Therefore, in two spins we are ahead 12 units, or six units per spin. We would soon own the casino. Naturally, we would take any kind of win, even one unit per spin. Thus, if the dealer were able to hit our 12 pockets three times every eight spins we would average 1.5 units per spin as a win (lose

12, lose 12, lose 12, lose 12, lose 12, win 35 -11, win 35 -11, win
35 - 11 = 12 units = +1.5 units per spin). Let's look at two dealers, A and B. We'll always count the numbers clockwise on a
double-zero wheel for the purposes of this illustration.

| Spin # | Distance from Last Number | |
	Dealer A	Dealer B
1	8	8
2	11	15
3	6	2
4	13	25
5	8	17
6	7	7
7	9	32
8	5	13
9	7	34
10	20	1
11	10	19
12	8	4
13	23	37
14	6	8
15	10	22
16	11	3
17	7	20
18	9	1
19	4	18
20	8	7

Let us take a look at Dealer A first. His spins range from
a low of four pockets away to a high of 23 pockets away. Four
of his 20 hits were eight spaces away; three of his 20 hits were
seven spaces away; two of his 20 hits were six spaces away.
We see that the overwhelming majority (18) of the 20 hits are
four to 13 pockets away from the last hit. That's 10 pockets
that we would bet. If this dealer continues to drop the ball in
a four to 13 pocket distance from the last hit nine of every 10
spins, we would not only own the casino in short order, we
would own the world. Unfortunately, I made up the distances
for dealer A (surprise!) and I doubt if you would find a dealer
with such a marked signature outside of my dreams. Dealer B

on the other hand is a different matter. He's real. But does he have a potential signature? Let's see.

Dealer B's total range is one to 37 pockets. Here we see distances of 1, 7 and 8 hitting twice plus distances of 2, 3 and 4 hitting once. Therefore nine of the 20 spins are within eight pockets of the last hit (one through eight pockets). Thus, your bet would be eight units on pockets distancing one to eight from the last number that hit. Dealer B existed in the *real* world, I didn't have to dream him up. If dealer B continued to hit within one to eight pockets 45% of the time, we might also find ourselves on easy street. Once again I must give a caution. Since we're only looking at 20 spins, many dealers will appear to have signatures because 20 spins is a very small number. Like biased-wheel play, to truly ascertain a dealer signature would take thousands of spins and, as I stated previously, such a study for determining the existence of dealer signatures seems doomed to failure by the mere fact of its undertaking. Correspondingly, even if you are playing a dealer with a pronounced signature, you might find that signature changing as the speed of the wheel changes. You would therefore have to slightly alter your betting pattern to correspond to the changing signature.

Long, Medium and Short Signatures

The above examples are each considered long signatures as they cover between eight and 12 distances from the last pockets. However, not all potential signatures would fall into a long pattern. Some dealers might have several different signature hits: for example three or four hits in a three-pocket distance, three or four hits in another three-pocket group, still three or four more in another three-pocket group. Long signatures are usually eight or more pockets grouped in succession, medium signatures are groupings of four to seven and short signatures are groupings of three or fewer. You might find a dealer hitting several times 10 pockets away from the last hit and several times 33 pockets away. You would then bet distances of 8, 9, 10, 11 and 12 pockets; and distances of 31, 32, 33,

34 and 35 pockets. Here's another thing to keep in mind: if the dealer is really consistent with his spins, you should start to make money *immediately*. If you find that a signature you're betting on starts to lose (perhaps because the wheel is slowing down imperceptibly), then move on to another dealer or re-calculate the signature. How many spins should you stay before moving? Considering that you are betting up to 12 and sometimes more numbers on a given spin, if you aren't winning an average of one in three (which is essentially a break-even proposition) then move on and analyze another dealer.

The following table will make it easy to calculate which pockets are a given distance from any number. When analyzing a dealer for a potential signature, simply place a ruler across the numbers to see their exact distance from the previous hit.

Double-Zero Wheel
Distance from last hit

Distance of pockets	# 0	# 1	# 2	# 3	# 4	# 5	# 6	# 7	# 8	# 9
1.	**28**	*00*	*0*	**24**	23	**22**	21	**20**	19	**26**
2.	9	27	**28**	36	**35**	34	**33**	32	**31**	30
3.	**26**	**10**	9	**13**	14	**15**	16	**17**	18	**11**
4.	30	25	**26**	1	**2**	3	**4**	5	**6**	7
5.	**11**	**29**	30	*00*	*0*	**24**	23	**22**	21	**20**
6.	7	12	**11**	27	**28**	36	**35**	34	**33**	32
7.	**20**	**8**	7	**10**	9	**13**	14	**15**	16	**17**
8.	32	19	**20**	25	**26**	1	**2**	3	**4**	5
9.	**17**	**31**	32	**29**	30	*00*	*0*	**24**	23	**22**
10.	5	18	**17**	12	**11**	27	**28**	36	**35**	34
11.	**22**	**6**	5	**8**	7	**10**	9	**13**	14	**15**
12.	34	21	**22**	19	**20**	25	**26**	1	**2**	3
13.	**15**	**33**	34	**31**	32	**29**	30	*00*	*0*	**24**
14.	3	16	**15**	18	**17**	12	**11**	27	**28**	36
15.	**24**	**4**	3	**6**	5	**8**	7	**10**	9	**13**
16.	36	23	**24**	21	**22**	19	**20**	25	**26**	1
17.	**13**	**35**	36	**33**	34	**31**	32	**29**	30	*00*
18.	1	14	**13**	16	**15**	18	**17**	12	**11**	27
19.	*00*	**2**	1	**4**	3	**6**	5	**8**	7	**10**
20.	27	*0*	*00*	23	**24**	21	**22**	19	**20**	25
21.	**10**	**28**	27	**35**	36	**33**	34	**31**	32	**29**
22.	25	9	**10**	14	**13**	16	**15**	18	**17**	12
23.	**29**	**26**	25	**2**	1	**4**	3	**6**	5	**8**
24.	12	30	**29**	*0*	*00*	23	**24**	21	**22**	19
25.	**8**	**11**	12	**28**	27	**35**	36	**33**	34	**31**
26.	19	7	**8**	9	**10**	14	**13**	16	**15**	18
27.	**31**	**20**	19	**26**	25	**2**	1	**4**	3	**6**
28.	18	32	**31**	30	**29**	*0*	*00*	23	**24**	21
29.	**6**	**17**	18	**11**	12	**28**	27	**35**	36	**33**
30.	21	5	**6**	7	**8**	9	**10**	14	**13**	16
31.	**33**	**22**	21	**20**	19	**26**	25	**2**	1	**4**
32.	16	34	**33**	32	**31**	30	**29**	*0*	*00*	23
33.	**4**	**15**	16	**17**	18	**11**	12	**28**	27	**35**
34.	23	3	**4**	5	**6**	7	**8**	9	**10**	14
35.	**35**	**24**	23	**22**	21	**20**	19	**26**	25	**2**
36.	14	36	**35**	34	**33**	32	**31**	30	**29**	*0*
37.	**2**	**13**	14	**15**	16	**17**	18	**11**	12	**28**
38.	*0*	1	**2**	3	**4**	5	**6**	7	**8**	9

Double-Zero Wheel
Distance from last hit

Distance of pockets	# 10	# 11	# 12	# 13	# 14	# 15	# 16	# 17	# 18	# 19
1.	25	7	8	1	2	3	4	5	6	31
2.	29	20	19	00	0	24	23	22	21	18
3.	12	32	31	27	28	36	35	34	33	6
4.	8	17	18	10	9	13	14	15	16	21
5.	19	5	6	25	26	1	2	3	4	33
6.	31	22	21	29	30	0	0	24	23	16
7.	18	34	33	12	11	27	28	36	35	4
8.	6	15	16	8	7	10	9	13	14	23
9.	21	3	4	19	20	25	26	1	2	35
10.	33	24	23	31	32	29	30	00	0	14
11.	16	36	35	18	17	12	11	27	28	2
12.	4	13	14	6	5	8	7	10	9	0
13.	23	1	2	21	22	19	20	25	26	28
14.	35	00	0	33	34	31	32	29	30	9
15.	14	27	28	16	15	18	17	12	11	26
16.	2	10	9	4	3	6	5	8	7	30
17.	0	25	26	23	24	21	22	19	20	11
18.	28	29	30	35	36	33	34	31	32	7
19.	9	12	11	14	13	16	15	18	17	20
20.	26	8	7	2	1	4	3	6	5	32
21.	30	19	20	0	00	23	24	21	22	17
22.	11	31	32	28	27	35	36	33	34	5
23.	7	18	17	9	10	14	13	16	15	22
24.	20	6	5	26	25	2	1	4	3	34
25.	32	21	22	30	29	0	00	23	24	15
26.	17	33	34	11	12	28	27	35	36	3
27.	5	16	15	7	8	9	10	14	13	24
28.	22	4	3	20	19	26	25	2	1	36
29.	34	23	24	32	31	30	29	00	00	13
30.	15	35	36	17	18	11	12	28	27	1
31.	3	14	13	5	6	7	8	9	10	00
32.	24	2	1	22	21	20	19	26	25	27
33.	36	0	00	34	33	32	31	30	29	10
34.	13	28	27	15	16	17	18	11	12	25
35.	1	9	10	3	4	5	6	7	8	29
36.	00	26	25	24	23	22	21	20	19	12
37.	27	30	29	36	35	34	33	32	31	8
38.	10	11	12	13	14	15	16	17	18	19

Double-Zero Wheel
Distance from last hit

Distance of pockets	# 20	# 21	# 22	# 23	# 24	# 25	# 26	# 27	# 28	# 29
1.	32	33	34	35	36	29	30	10	9	12
2.	17	16	15	14	13	12	11	25	26	8
3.	5	4	3	2	1	8	7	29	30	19
4.	22	23	24	0	00	19	20	12	11	31
5.	34	35	36	28	27	31	32	8	7	18
6.	15	14	13	9	10	18	17	19	20	6
7.	3	2	1	26	25	6	5	31	32	21
8.	24	0	00	30	29	21	22	18	17	33
9.	36	28	27	11	12	33	34	6	5	16
10.	13	9	10	7	8	16	15	21	22	4
11.	1	26	25	20	19	4	3	33	34	23
12.	00	30	29	32	31	23	24	16	15	35
13.	27	11	12	17	18	35	36	4	3	14
14.	10	7	8	5	6	14	13	23	24	2
15.	25	20	19	22	21	2	1	35	36	0
16.	29	32	31	34	33	0	00	14	13	28
17.	12	17	18	15	16	28	27	2	1	9
18.	8	5	6	3	4	9	10	0	00	26
19.	19	22	21	24	23	26	25	28	27	30
20.	31	34	33	36	35	30	29	9	10	11
21.	18	15	16	13	14	11	12	26	25	7
22.	6	3	4	1	2	7	8	30	29	20
23.	21	24	23	00	0	20	19	11	12	32
24.	33	36	35	27	28	32	31	7	8	17
25.	16	13	14	10	9	17	18	20	19	5
26.	4	1	2	25	26	5	6	32	31	22
27.	23	00	0	29	30	22	21	17	18	34
28.	35	27	28	12	11	34	33	5	6	15
29.	14	10	9	8	7	15	16	22	21	3
30.	2	25	26	19	20	3	4	34	33	24
31.	0	29	30	31	32	24	23	15	16	36
32.	28	12	11	18	17	36	35	3	4	13
33.	9	8	7	6	5	13	14	24	23	1
34.	26	19	20	21	22	1	2	36	35	00
35.	30	31	32	33	34	00	0	13	14	27
36.	11	18	17	16	15	27	28	1	2	10
37.	7	6	5	4	3	10	9	00	0	25
38.	20	21	22	23	24	25	26	27	28	29

Double-Zero Wheel
Distance from last hit

Distance of pockets	# 30	# 31	# 32	# 33	# 34	# 35	# 36	# 00
1.	11	18	17	16	15	14	13	27
2.	7	6	5	4	3	2	1	10
3.	20	21	22	23	24	0	00	25
4.	32	33	34	35	36	28	27	29
5.	17	16	15	14	13	9	10	12
6.	5	4	3	2	1	26	25	8
7.	22	23	24	0	00	30	29	19
8.	34	35	36	28	27	11	12	31
9.	15	14	13	9	10	7	8	18
10.	3	2	1	26	25	20	19	6
11.	24	0	00	30	29	32	31	21
12.	36	28	27	11	12	17	18	33
13.	13	9	10	7	8	5	6	16
14.	1	26	25	20	19	22	21	4
15.	00	30	29	32	31	34	33	23
16.	27	11	12	17	18	15	16	35
17.	10	7	8	5	6	3	4	14
18.	25	20	19	22	21	24	23	2
19.	29	32	31	34	33	36	35	0
20.	12	17	18	15	16	13	14	28
21.	8	5	6	3	4	1	2	9
22.	19	22	21	24	23	00	0	26
23.	31	34	33	36	35	27	28	30
24.	18	15	16	13	14	10	9	11
25.	6	3	4	1	2	25	26	7
26.	21	24	23	00	0	29	30	20
27.	33	36	35	27	28	12	11	32
28.	16	13	14	10	9	8	7	17
29.	4	1	2	25	26	19	20	5
30.	23	00	0	29	30	31	32	22
31.	35	27	28	12	11	18	17	34
32.	14	10	9	8	7	6	5	15
33.	2	25	26	19	20	21	22	3
34.	0	29	30	31	32	33	34	24
35.	28	12	11	18	17	16	15	36
36.	9	8	7	6	5	4	3	13
37.	26	19	20	21	22	23	24	1
38.	30	31	32	33	34	35	36	00

Single-Zero Wheel
Distance from last hit

Distance of pockets	# 0	# 1	# 2	# 3	# 4	# 5	# 6	# 7	# 8	# 9
1.	32	20	25	26	21	24	27	28	23	22
2.	15	14	17	0	2	16	13	12	10	18
3.	19	31	34	32	25	33	36	35	5	29
4.	4	9	6	15	17	1	11	3	24	7
5.	21	22	27	19	34	20	30	26	16	28
6.	2	18	13	4	6	14	8	0	33	12
7.	25	29	36	21	27	31	23	32	1	35
8.	17	7	11	2	13	9	10	15	20	3
9.	34	28	30	25	36	22	5	19	14	26
10.	6	12	8	17	11	18	24	4	31	0
11.	27	35	23	34	30	29	16	21	9	32
12.	13	3	10	6	8	7	33	2	22	15
13.	36	26	5	27	23	28	1	25	18	19
14.	11	0	24	13	10	12	20	17	29	4
15.	30	32	16	36	5	35	14	34	7	21
16.	8	15	33	11	24	3	31	6	28	2
17.	23	19	1	30	16	26	9	27	12	25
18.	10	4	20	8	33	0	22	13	35	17
19.	5	21	14	23	1	32	18	36	3	34
20.	24	2	31	10	20	15	29	11	26	6
21.	16	25	9	5	14	19	7	30	0	27
22.	33	17	22	24	31	4	28	8	32	13
23.	1	34	18	16	9	21	12	23	15	36
24.	20	6	29	33	22	2	35	10	19	11
25.	14	27	7	1	18	25	3	5	4	30
26.	31	13	28	20	29	17	26	24	21	8
27.	9	36	12	14	7	34	0	16	2	23
28.	22	11	35	31	28	6	32	33	25	10
29.	18	30	3	9	12	27	15	1	17	5
30.	29	8	26	22	35	13	19	20	34	24
31.	7	23	0	18	3	36	4	14	6	16
32.	28	10	32	29	26	11	21	31	27	33
33.	12	5	15	7	0	30	2	9	13	1
34.	35	24	19	28	32	8	25	22	36	20
35.	3	16	4	12	15	23	17	18	11	14
36.	26	33	21	35	19	10	34	29	30	31
37.	0	1	2	3	4	5	6	7	8	9

Single-Zero Wheel
Distance from last hit

Distance of pockets	# 10	# 11	# 12	# 13	# 14	# 15	# 16	# 17	# 18	# 19
1.	5	30	35	36	31	19	33	34	29	4
2.	24	8	3	11	9	4	1	6	7	21
3.	16	23	26	30	22	21	20	27	28	2
4.	33	10	0	8	18	2	14	13	12	25
5.	1	5	32	23	29	25	31	36	35	17
6.	20	24	15	10	7	17	9	11	3	34
7.	14	16	19	5	28	34	22	30	26	6
8.	31	33	4	24	12	6	18	8	0	27
9.	9	1	21	16	35	27	29	23	32	13
10.	22	20	2	33	3	13	7	10	15	36
11.	18	14	25	1	26	36	28	5	19	11
12.	29	31	17	20	0	11	12	24	4	30
13.	7	9	34	14	32	30	35	16	21	8
14.	28	22	6	31	15	8	3	33	2	23
15.	12	18	27	9	19	23	26	1	25	10
16.	35	29	13	22	4	10	0	20	17	5
17.	3	7	36	18	21	5	32	14	34	24
18.	26	28	11	29	2	24	15	31	6	16
19.	0	12	30	7	25	16	19	9	27	33
20.	32	35	8	28	17	33	4	22	13	1
21.	15	3	23	12	34	1	21	18	36	20
22.	19	26	10	35	6	20	2	29	11	14
23.	4	0	5	3	27	14	25	7	30	31
24.	21	32	24	26	13	31	17	28	8	9
25.	2	15	16	0	36	9	34	12	23	22
26.	25	19	33	32	11	22	6	35	10	18
27.	17	4	1	15	30	18	27	3	5	29
28.	34	21	20	19	8	29	13	26	24	7
29.	6	2	14	4	23	7	36	0	16	28
30.	27	25	31	21	10	28	11	32	33	12
31.	13	17	9	2	5	12	30	15	1	35
32.	36	34	22	24	24	35	8	19	20	3
33.	11	6	18	17	16	3	23	4	14	26
34.	30	27	29	34	33	26	10	21	31	0
35.	8	13	7	6	1	0	5	2	9	32
36.	23	36	28	27	20	3 2	24	25	22	15
37.	10	11	12	13	14	15	16	17	18	19

Single-Zero Wheel
Distance from last hit

Distance of pockets	# 20	# 21	# 22	# 23	# 24	# 25	# 26	# 27	# 28	# 29
1.	14	2	18	10	16	17	0	13	12	7
2.	31	25	29	5	33	34	32	36	35	28
3.	9	17	7	24	1	6	15	11	3	12
4.	22	34	28	16	20	27	19	30	26	35
5.	18	6	12	33	14	13	4	8	0	3
6.	29	27	35	1	31	36	21	23	32	26
7.	7	13	3	20	9	11	2	10	15	0
8.	28	36	26	14	22	30	25	5	19	32
9.	12	11	0	31	18	8	17	24	4	15
10.	35	30	32	9	29	23	34	16	21	19
11.	3	8	15	22	7	10	6	33	2	4
12.	26	23	19	18	28	5	27	1	25	21
13.	0	10	4	29	12	24	13	20	17	2
14.	32	5	21	7	35	16	36	14	34	25
15.	15	24	2	28	3	33	11	31	6	17
16.	19	16	25	12	26	1	30	9	27	34
17.	4	33	17	35	0	20	8	22	13	6
18.	21	1	34	3	32	14	23	18	36	27
19.	2	20	6	26	15	31	10	29	11	13
20.	25	14	27	0	19	9	5	7	30	36
21.	17	31	13	32	4	22	24	28	8	11
22.	34	9	36	15	21	18	16	12	23	30
23.	6	22	11	19	2	29	33	35	10	8
24.	27	18	30	4	25	7	1	3	5	23
25.	13	29	8	21	17	28	20	26	24	10
26.	36	7	23	2	34	12	14	0	16	5
27.	11	28	10	25	6	35	31	32	33	24
28.	30	12	5	17	27	3	9	15	1	16
29.	8	35	24	34	13	26	22	19	20	33
30.	23	3	16	6	36	0	18	4	14	1
31.	10	26	33	27	11	32	29	21	31	20
32.	5	0	1	13	30	15	7	2	9	14
33.	24	32	20	36	8	19	28	25	22	31
34.	16	15	14	11	23	4	12	17	18	9
35.	33	19	31	30	10	21	35	34	29	22
36.	1	4	9	8	5	2	3	6	7	18
37.	20	21	22	23	24	25	26	27	28	29

Single-Zero Wheel
Distance from last hit

Distance of pockets	# 30	# 31	# 32	# 33	# 34	# 35	# 36
1.	8	9	15	1	6	3	11
2.	23	22	19	20	27	26	30
3.	10	18	4	14	13	0	8
4.	5	29	21	31	36	32	23
5.	24	7	2	9	11	15	10
6.	16	28	25	22	30	19	5
7.	33	12	17	18	8	4	24
8.	1	35	34	29	23	21	16
9.	20	3	6	7	10	2	33
10.	14	26	27	28	5	25	1
11.	31	0	13	12	24	17	20
12.	9	32	36	35	16	34	14
13.	22	15	11	3	33	6	31
14.	18	19	30	26	1	27	9
15.	29	4	8	0	20	13	22
16.	7	21	23	32	14	36	18
17.	28	2	10	15	31	11	29
18.	12	25	5	19	9	30	7
19.	35	17	24	4	22	8	28
20.	3	34	16	21	18	23	12
21.	26	6	33	2	29	10	35
22.	0	27	1	25	7	5	3
23.	32	13	20	17	28	24	26
24.	15	36	14	34	12	16	0
25.	19	11	31	6	35	33	32
26.	4	30	9	27	3	1	15
27.	21	8	22	13	26	20	19
28.	2	23	18	36	0	14	4
29.	25	10	29	11	32	31	21
30.	17	5	7	30	15	9	2
31.	34	24	28	8	19	22	25
32.	6	16	12	23	4	18	17
33.	27	33	35	10	21	29	34
34.	13	1	3	5	2	7	6
35.	36	20	26	24	25	28	27
36.	11	14	0	16	17	12	13
37.	30	31	32	33	34	35	36

The following are scoreboards from various casinos. One dealer has spun the ball for each of the recorded hits. Let's see how we would play these scoreboards based on potential dealer signatures.

SCOREBOARD # 1:

Number	Distance from last pocket	
34	....	
18	16	**Low:** 2 pockets
15	23	**High:** 36 pockets
32	33	
14	28	**Multiple Hits:**
0	2	2 pockets 3 times
00	19	4 pockets 2 times
10	2	29 pockets 2 times
20	24	
8	18	**Groups:**
6	4	7 hits = 2 to 8 pockets
4	4	6 hits = 28 to 36 pockets
28	6	
2	36	**Bet:**
18	29	Seven numbers: 2 through 8
00	34	pockets away from last hit
10	2	and two numbers 28 and 29
34	29	pockets away from last hit.
27	8	
21	10	**Total:** 9 units

SCOREBOARD # 2:

Number	Distance from last pocket
8	....
18	3
17	19
34	3
00	7
31	8
12	35
24	29
33	16
15	20
34	37
16	20
9	8
34	10
15	1
27	7
19	6
34	24
12	12
0	14

Low: 1 pocket
High: 37 pockets

Multiple Hits:
3 pockets 2 times
7 pockets 2 times
8 pockets 2 times
20 pockets 2 times

Groups:
9 hits 1 to 10 pockets
10 hits 1 to 12 pockets
3 hits 19 and 20 pockets

Bet:
Ten numbers 1 to 10 pockets away from last hit and two numbers 19 and 20 pockets away from last hit.

Total: 12 units

SCOREBOARD # 3:

Number	Distance from last pocket	
27	....	
22	29	**Low:** 1 pocket
31	16	**High:** 37 pockets
9	13	
32	9	**Multiple Hits:**
17	1	16 pockets 2 times
29	14	14 pockets 2 times
22	26	
10	10	**Groups:**
28	18	10 hits 9 to 18 pockets
24	14	3 hits 29, 30, 31 pockets
3	37	
22	35	**Bet:**
31	16	Bet ten numbers 9 to 18 pockets
16	5	away from last hit and three
17	15	numbers 29, 30, 31 pockets away
21	21	from last hit.
25	30	
4	11	**Total:** 13 units
19	3	

SCOREBOARD # 4:

Number	Distance from last pocket
18	....
7	16
22	5
11	32
16	27
19	32
22	23
35	24
9	5
34	10
36	4
4	17
0	5
6	29
21	1
23	4
28	5
34	11
27	8

Low: 1 pocket
High: 32 pockets

Multiple Hits:
5 pockets 4 times
32 pockets 3 times
4 pockets 2 times

Groups:
8 hits 1 to 8 pockets
4 hits 29 to 32 pockets

Bet:
Bet eight numbers 1 to 8 pockets away from last hit and four numbers 29 to 32 hits away from last hit.

Total: 12 units

SCOREBOARD # 5:

Number	Distance from last pocket
21	....
13	25
3	35
00	5
28	20
0	37
00	19
10	2
28	18
18	27
12	34
9	16
00	17
3	33
4	19
18	33
18	38
32	18
3	25
32	32

Low: 2 pockets
High: 38 pockets

Multiple Hits:
19 pockets 2 times
33 pockets 2 times
25 pockets 2 times
18 pockets 2 times

Groups:
7 hits 16 to 20 pockets
5 hits 25 to 33 pockets

Bet:
Bet five numbers 16 to 20 pockets away from last hit and one unit each on numbers 25 and 33 pockets away from last hit.

Total: 7 units

SCOREBOARD # 6:

Number	Distance from last pocket
5	....
30	32
4	29
7	11
9	34
18	26
21	2
10	29
23	13
11	9
24	10
32	31
23	26
14	2
00	21
4	14
18	33
32	18
17	1
19	17

Low: 1 pocket

High: 34 pockets

Multiple Hits:
29 pockets 2 times
26 pockets 2 times
2 pockets 2 times

Groups:
8 hits 26 to 34 pockets
3 hits 1 to 2 pockets

Bet:
Bet nine numbers 26 to 34 pockets
away from last hit and two
numbers 1 to 2 pockets away
from last hit.

Total: 11 units

SCOREBOARD # 7:

Number	Distance from last pocket	
36	....	**Low:** 2 pockets
24	37	**High:** 38 pockets
13	2	
25	5	**Multiple Hits:**
18	6	37 pockets 3 times
26	13	12 pockets 2 times
25	19	
25	38	**Groups:**
32	24	4 hits 37 and 38 pockets
23	26	4 hits 12 to 15 pockets
22	15	5 hits 22 to 26 pockets
1	7	
21	12	**Bet:**
3	22	Bet two numbers 37 and 38
15	37	pockets away from last hit, four
11	30	numbers 12 to 15 pockets away
18	23	from last hit, and five numbers 22
31	37	to 26 pockets away from last hit.
28	12	
19	25	**Total:** 11 units

SCOREBOARD # 8:

Number	Distance from last pocket
29	....
17	24
1	9
16	14
31	33
23	7
15	17
17	34
9	31
21	28
10	29
4	12
36	21
22	33
00	8
3	33
28	25
32	7
17	1
2	28

Low: 1 pocket

High: 34 pockets

Multiple Hits:

33 pockets 3 times

7 pockets 2 times

28 pockets 2 times

Groups:

8 hits 28 to 34 pockets

4 hits 7 to 9 pockets

Bet:

Bet seven numbers 28 to 34 pockets away from last hit and three numbers 7 to 9 pockets away from last hit.

Total: 10 units

SCOREBOARD # 9:

Number	Distance from last pocket
34	....
4	21
17	14
14	27
14	38
5	12
15	3
15	38
17	34
29	14
22	26
25	11
34	28
32	34
23	26
3	18
15	37
18	15
0	10
17	9

Low: 3 pockets

High: 38 pockets

Multiple Hits:
14 pockets 2 times
38 pockets 2 times
34 pockets 2 times
26 pockets 2 times

Groups:
9 hits 26 to 38 pockets
7 hits 9 to 14 pockets

Bet:
Bet 13 numbers 26 to 38 pockets away from last hit.

Total: 13 units

SCOREBOARD # 10:

Number	Distance from last pocket
27	....
2	17
4	34
29	28
20	22
21	23
26	11
7	3
29	17
8	2
35	10
5	13
2	27
17	10
7	35
9	34
0	36
28	1
34	11
33	19

Low: 1 pocket
High: 36 pockets

Multiple Hits:
17 pockets 2 times
34 pockets 2 times
11 pockets 2 times
10 pockets 2 times

Groups:
7 hits 10 to 17 pockets
4 hits 34 to 36 pockets

Bet:
Bet eight numbers 10 to 17 pockets away from last hit and three numbers 34 to 36 pockets away from last hit.

Total: 11 units

SCOREBOARD # 11:

Number	Distance from last pocket
35	....
6	32
34	21
2	25
14	37
5	12
11	33
0	33
3	14
26	27
26	38
0	35
14	36
14	38
27	22
16	12
1	24
5	30
9	30
10	19

Low: 12 pockets
High: 38 pockets

Multiple Hits:
12 pockets 2 times
33 pockets 2 times
38 pockets 2 times
30 pockets 2 times

Groups:
10 hits 30 to 38 pockets
3 hits 12 to 14 pockets

Bet:
Bet nine numbers 30 to 38 pockets away from last hit and three numbers 12 to 14 pockets away from last hit.

Total: 12 units

SCOREBOARD # 12:

Number	Distance from last pocket	
5	....	
16	22	**Low:** 1 pocket
32	14	**High:** 37 pockets
0	30	
30	4	**Multiple Hits:**
2	33	8 pockets 2 times
32	9	1 pocket 2 times
20	37	
24	8	**Groups:**
9	25	7 hits 1 to 9 pockets
3	12	4 hits 12 to 16 pockets
31	13	
24	26	**Bet:**
29	8	Bet nine numbers 1 to 9 pockets
36	31	away from last hit and five
13	1	numbers 12 to 16 pockets away
1	1	from last hit.
32	28	
24	7	**Total:** 14 units
33	16	

Scobe's Wager:
The Last Word in the Hunt for the Unicorns of Roulette

The fact that we can't really prove one way or the other that sector shooting or dealer signatures exist should not bother the recreational roulette player. The simple fact is that the recreational roulette player is going to play roulette *no matter what.* So if you fit the recreational profile — the "I love roulette and I'm going to play it no matter what the odds that I face" — then you have nothing to lose and *everything to gain* by playing sections or signatures. What I am offering you is my version of *Pascal's Wager.*

The French mathematician and philosopher Blaise Pascal (1623-1662), commenting on whether one should believe in God or not, stated that it is better to function as if God exists, rather than as if He didn't exist, for the following reason: If God doesn't exist but you live as if he does, when you die, no harm done — you cease to exist, that's all. However, if God does exist and you live as if He doesn't exist (thus denying Him and violating His laws) — you're in hot water, or fire, when you die! Thus, live as if God exists and all will be right with you in the now and in the hereafter, regardless of whether God actually does exist or not. *Scobe's Wager* can be formulated thusly: Play *as if* section-shooting dealers exist, and play *as if* dealers have signatures because if they don't, no harm done, but if they do — well, you might find yourself in roulette heaven.

8

Chameleon Roulette:

How to Mimic Fortune's Favorites

In *The Julian Strategies in Roulette* (Paone Press), John F. Julian recounts an inadvertent meeting with a visual wheel clocker at the Mirage in Las Vegas. A visual wheel tracker or dealer tracker watches the ball and predicts — by sight — which sector of the wheel the ball will fall into. Here's Julian's account:

> I once saw a wealthy, fashionably-dressed, heavily made-up but downright glamorous woman at the Mirage in Las Vegas win four bets in a row at roulette — on four different numbers! She was squealing with delight and her companion, a sallow young man who seemed frustrated, just smirked and told the crowd of onlookers: "She does this all the time. I've lost a small fortune at roulette and all she does is win. I should bet with her. But I've got my own lucky numbers."
>
> Two spins later, the woman hit another number which was attested to by her squeals of delight. As soon as the sallow young man had lamented his woe, I wondered why he hadn't bet with her. I also watched the young

woman closely. She never placed a bet until the ball was actually spun and after it had made several revolutions. When
she put down her bets, usually three or four numbers, I put
down $25 on the same numbers. On the first spin, I lost my
$100. On the second spin, one of my three numbers hit. I
was $725 richer. . . .

The woman was a *visual wheel tracker*. She was able to
anticipate with an incredible degree of accuracy, where the
ball was going to fall.

Dr. Olaf Vancura in his excellent general volume on gambling, *Smart Casino Gambling* (Index Publishing Group), also
records an unusual experience with a visual tracker.

> An interesting occurrence of possible Dealer Tracking
> occurred a few years ago in the Trop World casino in At-
> lantic City. . . . I was making my way to an exit but hap-
> pened to notice an individual playing at one of the Roulette
> tables. Actually, what I happened to notice was the huge
> stack of chips in front of him. Not only did he have about
> 100 grey chips, but he had roughly $4,000 of regular casino
> chips as well . . .
>
> What I witnessed that evening was a most interesting
> series of events. The gentleman, whom for lack of a better
> moniker I shall refer to as Mr. Grey, seemed to make only in-
> dividual bets of $25 each on 8 or 9 numbers at a time. Unlike
> the others at the table, he would begin to place his bets only
> after the dealer spun the ball. I watched Mr. Grey for about
> 10 minutes, during which time he won twice.
>
> My curiosity aroused, I moved closer to look at his
> method. I began to notice that the numbers on which he bet
> were not chosen by chance. For each spin, the numbers on
> which he bet fell within one sector, or section, of the rotor. I
> now realized that somehow Mr. Grey was predicting, or at
> least he believed he was predicting, in which portion of the
> wheel the ball would ultimately land.
>
> The dealer took a break, and Mr. Grey inquired if she'd
> be back soon. The dealer replied that she would return in 20
> minutes. . . . As the new dealer started, Mr. Grey altered his
> strategy. He now began to wager the table minimum and
> only on Red and Black bets. . . .
>
> This continued until the original dealer returned. At
> this point, Mr. Grey again began betting heavily on sectors.

I watched for another 15 minutes as Mr. Grey netted an additional $500. . . . Mr. Grey cashed in his chips to the tune of some $8,000. After his departure, I inquired and was told by the pit boss that a little over one hour ago Mr. Grey had bought $5,000 worth of chips. So Mr. Grey made $3,000 for one hour's "work."

The point of the above two stories is not to prove the validity of visual wheel trackers or visual dealer trackers — Laurance Scott has sufficiently handled that topic and talent (see Chapter Nine) — but to indicate a possible way to take advantage of individuals who have this skill or, just as importantly, a possible way to take advantage of individuals who have tracked a wheel for thousands of spins, ascertained that it is biased, and are now betting the bias. In fact, this chapter will make you a "gambling parasite" as you'll be feeding on other people's luck, skill, and/or talent. Someone else's good fortune could become your good fortune too! Of course, if the parasite imagery disgusts you, then you can think of yourself as a chameleon, mimicking the shades of the bettors who are flush with winning.

The Chameleon Strategy is simple and straightforward: Look for someone who is winning and bet with him or her. If she/he and you continue to win, then continue to do what you've been doing — follow that person's betting lead. If she/he and you start to lose, leave the person flat and go find someone else to bet with (sorry, loyalty is not a good trait in this strategy). There are generally six reasons for why someone is winning at a roulette table:

1. The person is experiencing luck — pure, blind and dumb luck.
2. The person is a biased-wheel player and has been betting and winning on the bias.
3. The person is working with a sector-shooting dealer who is placing the ball in sectors that his partner is betting on.
4. The person has discovered the dealer's signature and is betting it.
5. The person is a visual wheel tracker and can judge

with a good degree of accuracy in what sector of the wheel the ball will land.

6. The person is using a computer to determine where the ball will fall (see Chapter Nine).

In truth, most of the people who are winning at roulette at any given table or casino on any given shift or day are merely the beneficiaries of Lady Luck's largesse. Still, as *Scobe's Wager* states — you can't hurt yourself by playing this strategy because if the person is *only* lucky — well, they are still winning! You might win, too.

You might lose, too, of course. But you have not increased your chances of losing just because someone has been lucky for the past several spins or past several hours. As we know, the game doesn't run like that. Roulette is an independent trial game — the ball and wheel have no memories and therefore don't have to make up for past events. The lucky person can continue being lucky. The unlucky person can continue being unlucky. That's on an unbiased wheel.

The brightest chameleon scenario is that you are mimicking a person from groups two through six. If so, then you will be playing a game that now favors you over the casino. Isn't that everyone's dream — a windfall sans working for it? By mimicking winning players' wagers, you have a decent shot of occasionally stumbling on individuals who make killings at the tables. Note that of the two examples at the opening of this chapter, one, Julian, started to bet with the "lucky lady" and he even won some money. Follow his lead and you might win, too.

How to Clock Players

Julian has delineated ten things to watch for when "looking for the lucky lady or fortunate fella" as he calls the Chameleon Strategy. In essence, this strategy is a player-clocking strategy. With Julian's permission, I have paraphrased and expanded on his categories and commentary for the benefit of our discussion.

1. Look for someone who is winning. Obviously. However, don't take for granted that a huge pile of chips in front of a player indicates that he has been winning. It might just indicate that he has bought in for a lot or that his chips are valued at the minimum. When in doubt just ask: "So how's your luck running today?" If you don't want to bother the player, question the dealer ("That guy's doing well?") or another player at the table — although roulette players are notoriously single-minded about their own bets and might not know that someone else is hammering the casino.

2. Ask the other players, or one of the pit people, how long this person has been playing. The longer the person has been playing, the better the chance that he or she is not just lucky but a proficient wheel player of some sort. If the person has been playing two or more hours, then jump in and bet chameleon style. Roulette (especially double zero) has such a strong house edge that it tends to grind the average player rather quickly. A sustained winning streak is always possible by luck, granted, but it could be an indication that a player has done his homework.

3. See if the player is betting a sector of the wheel when placing bets. Is it always the same sector or does the player move the bets around? If it is the same sector, bet chameleon-style right away. If the player is moving bets around, try to figure out if there's a method to the movement. If it simply looks as if the player is taking pot shots, pass on by.

4. See if the player is betting a *single* number. Notice whether or not the player is keeping a record of every spin. If the player is doing this, try to see if he or she has any lists that were compiled earlier in the day, or on past days, in view. That would indicate that this particular player may have found a single biased number over an extended period of wheel clocking. If it seems as if this is the case, bet with the player.

5. Notice if the winning player is looking at another player at the table in a way that might indicate that they are communicating by signals. Does one player place a bet on a number and the winning player always place the

number next to it, three spaces down or up, etc.? If you
see this kind of pattern on five to 10 spins, you may have
uncovered a team. Bet with the winning player and join
the team. It is also possible that a player might be getting
signals from someone who is not actually playing or from
someone who is not even at the table. Look around. Is the
player in eye contact with someone nearby — or across
the room? You just might have uncovered someone playing with a computer tracking system. Join the computer
age (see Chapter Nine).

6. Notice whether the player is placing bets after the ball
has been spun. If so, see if the individual does this consistently on a given revolution. If the ball has only four or
five spins to go and then the player places a bet, it's quite
possible that this player is a visual wheel tracker. You're
now on the track team. Bet with him or her.

7. Take a good look at the people in the pit. Are they ner-
vous? Are they on the telephone a lot? Are they hovering
over the winning player trying to figure out the method
he or she is using? Or is the pit empty? Have all the pit
people suddenly vanished? That's a good sign that the
player is being observed by the "eye in the sky." So now
the "eye" can observe your bets, too.

8. Is the person who is winning on very friendly terms
with the pit personnel? If so, ask the pit people if this person wins like this all the time. If the pit people say yes,
most times, then become a chameleon. If the pit people
say no, he's just having a good run, consider becoming a
jackrabbit and hopping on by.

9. If you see someone standing and observing the wheel,
all the while scribbling down numbers, glance at the
sheet. Are certain numbers circled? Highlighted? Does it
appear that this individual is preparing to jump in and
bet? Wait a while and see if the player gets into the game.
Is the player betting the circled numbers on every spin? If
so, do so too. Even though the player has not yet won,
there's a decent chance that he or she is playing a bias that
has been found. By the way, the longer the list is that the
player is using, the better the chance that you have found
a truly biased wheel.

10. Is the winning player only winning when a certain dealer is running the game? When the dealer leaves, does the player who is winning take a break or reduce the size of his or her bets? If so, then you may have hit upon a dealer who has a conscious or unconscious signature, and a player who is using that signature to choose his or her bets. When the original dealer returns, does the player start to increase his or her bets? If so, bet with the player. Remember Vancura's incident in Atlantic City? Had he jumped in when the original dealer returned and Mr. Grey started to increase his bets, he might have made a little money.

Money Requirements for Chameleon Play

If you are going to play the chameleon way, you have to realize that the likelihood that any given winning player is an expert wheel tracker is decidedly remote. However, from my own informal research, I have discovered that there are more of these people out there than I had imagined. In Las Vegas and Atlantic City there are teams of biased-wheel trackers and visual wheel trackers. Playing the chameleon way also allows you to exploit those people who have stumbled on BIG numbers and biased wheels without them realizing it. In fact, it doesn't matter *why* or *how* some players have shifted the odds in their favor, it only matters that they have and that you are prepared to take advantage of it.

Still, we have to be prepared for the very real fact that often the luck will run dry and the chameleon player will start to lose. When is enough enough? I think 20 spins of a wheel is sufficient to give you an indication of whether it's time to move on or employ another strategy. If you give yourself a 20 spin limit, at the end of which you are behind, then make a move. However, if you are ahead after 20 spins of chameleon play, then stay for another 20 spins. As long as you're winning, stay. A simple rule — maybe the true golden rule — if you're winning stay and do unto the casinos what they wish they were doing unto you.

9

Odds and "Evends":

Everything You Ever Wanted to Know About Roulette (Well, Almost)

If you use the methods discussed in this book for biased wheel-play, or for short-term BIG Number or Sector Slicing (the double-dynamite roulette system), or for dealer signature tracking, or chameleon betting, you do have a chance to take home some money. Even my layout strategies, which make no pretense at long-term victory, can reduce your *exposure* to the house edge, lessen your overall losses, and still give you full playing pleasure. But there are some odds and ends to tie up. As with all gamblers, roulette players have many questions they want answered. In researching this book and giving seminars throughout the country on roulette and other games, I've talked to several hundred roulette players. These were the most frequently asked questions or pieces of information they wanted addressed.

I have heard about visual wheel tracking but I have never seen a book or article about it. Does it exist? If so, how is it done?

Visual wheel tracking is a technique developed and sold by Laurance Scott, a computer expert. The general idea of visual wheel tracking is that the human eye and mind are capable of figuring where the ball will land. The visual wheel tracker starts with the premise that no matter how many revolutions a ball takes around the wheel, the last few revolutions will be the same for all dealers, especially if the wheel is warped or old. It doesn't matter if the ball goes around a dozen times or two dozen times, the last four or five spins will behave in the same way. Laurance Scott calls this a "wheel signature" as opposed to a dealer signature. In order to win with this method, you have to discover a wheel where the final revolutions are uniform and know when and where to place your bets. You have to be able to figure when the last four or five spins are coming. You also have to be able to adjust your predictions to the various wheel speeds. Sound difficult? It is. Scott does not think that all players who attempt his technique will succeed. Just the opposite. His estimate is that maybe two to three percent of the roulette-playing public has the motivation and the "eye" for visual wheel tracking. For these players, some 40 hours or more of training is necessary to become somewhat proficient at the technique. Are there people doing this? Absolutely. Both John F. Julian and Olaf Vancura encountered them and Scott maintains that there are over 50 professional wheel trackers making the rounds. According to Scott, they play with upwards of a 40 percent edge over the casino. The only problem that develops for these trackers is the fact that the casino can easily thwart them by not allowing bets after the ball is spun or calling out "no more bets" before the last four or five spins. Such actions can wipe out the visual wheel tracker's whole game plan.

You say to follow the scoreboards to determine which numbers to bet. Boy are you right! I was walking by the roulette pits and the number 6 had hit all 20 times on a single scoreboard. The table was closed. Isn't that the most ever for one number to hit in a row? No wonder they closed the table.

If that number 6 had indeed hit 20 times in a row, it would be a once in a lifetime occurrence — perhaps a once in a million lifetimes' occurrence — a once in a universe's lifetime's occurrence. What you saw was not a table closed because one number was hitting with paranormal regularity but a table that was closed while the scoreboard was being reprogrammed. Generally, you will find this happening when the casinos are relatively empty, such as early morning. Sometimes scoreboards malfunction as well and are repaired or reprogrammed. This would also account for a number being on all 20 spots.

I saw the number 24 hit three times in a row. What are the odds of this happening?

The probability of any number hitting three times in a row on a double-zero wheel is once in 54,872 spins (38 X 38 X 38) for odds of 54,871 to one. Since every number has a one in 38 chance of coming up on a double-zero wheel, the probability is found by multiplying 38 X 38 for multiple hits. I was going to figure out what 38 hits of the same number in a row was but the number was too big to fit on my calculator! On a single-zero wheel three numbers have a slightly more favorable one in 50,653 chance of happening (37 X 37 X 37) which gives us odds of 50,652 to one.

What is the most any one number hit in a row?

This is hard to answer because there is no official record book (I think someone should start one) that has kept track of these things. However, according to Russell Barnhart, the number **10** appeared six times in a row on July 9th, 1959 at the El San Juan Hotel in Puerto Rico. The probability of this happening is once in 3,010,936,384 spins. In 1988, the number 23 occurred five times in a row in a German casino. The probability of that is once in 69,343,957 spins. I have personally seen a given number hit four times in a row once and three times in a row on a couple of occasions.

What is the most any one color or other even-money bet hit in a row?

Here we have the same problem as above. Except for an occasional magazine or newspaper story, we have no official record books. I witnessed a run of 14 blacks in a row and several runs of 12 (blacks or reds) in a row. I know someone who swears she saw 17 reds in a row. There is an unconfirmed report that a run of 28 "evens" in a row occurred at Monte Carlo in 1939. Again an official record book that kept track of these things would be a fun endeavor. We all like to read (and fantasize) about outlandish runs and record wins.

Who has won the most money playing roulette?

There have been quite a few big winners in roulette that we know about (and I'm sure many hundreds that we don't know about). Here are the top winning roulette players and/or teams, the total they have won, when they played, and where they played.

Name:	Won:	When:	Where:
1. Billy Walters Team	$4,810,000	1986-89	Las Vegas/ Atlantic City
2. Richard Jarecki	$1,280,000	1971	Monte Carlo/ San Remo
3. Unknown Team(s)	$ 600,000	1948-51	Mar del Plata
4. Helmut Berlin Team	$ 420,000	1951	Mar del Plata
5. Joseph Jaggers	$ 325,000	1873	Monte Carlo
6. Italian Team	$ 160,000	1880	Monte Carlo
7. Pierre Basieux Team	$ 153,000	1981	Bad Wiessee
8. Albert Hibbs/ Roy Walford	$ 40,000	1947-48	Las Vegas/ Reno
9. The Jones Boys Team	$ 32,000	1958	Las Vegas

I must mention that it is quite possible for someone to win big, only to lose some, much, most or all of it back. I've seen mega-rollers playing roulette in Las Vegas be up more than most of the people on this list, only to continue to play and fall victim to luck's vagaries. What makes the above list worthy of note is that to the best of my knowledge most of the players kept their wins (or a good portion of them) and went home winners.

How many total roulette wheels are there in the world?

As I write this, I estimate that there are approximately 5,000 roulette wheels in casinos across the world with more coming on-line every month as the casino boom continues. My guess is that by the time the casino boom levels off, we'll have approximately 6,000 to 8,000 wheels worldwide to choose from . . . and may they all be biased.

Where are the most roulette wheels found?

The United States has the most roulette wheels, followed by France and England. However, Europe has three times as many roulette wheels in operation as Canada and the United States combined.

I read a book about roulette that was published in England. There were maybe 50 different betting systems discussed. Yet, you talk about a handful of systems. What about all these others?

Some European books go into exhaustive detail concerning layout strategies (see Chapter Twelve) that can be employed but few of these books talk about real ways of beating roulette. Unfortunately, all the layout strategies are merely variations of the basic layout systems given in this book. For example, there is a system called "orphan play." This merely means betting on a number that hasn't appeared in a long time. Such a number is an "orphan" because it's been left out and, by betting it, you are now "adopting" it. Sometimes, this is called a sleeper bet because the number has been sleeping. Of course, if the number hasn't hit or is "sleeping" that means other numbers are hitting more than they should. Consider that you might be at a biased wheel. If you are, the orphan or sleeping number could be a *negative bias* and betting on it could be the worst of all possible approaches. In European roulette you will hear such impressive terms as Paroli, as in "I did a Paroli of three." This is a fancy name for increasing one's bet after a win, usually by doubling. In craps parlance, we call this a "press." While the vocabulary of gambling is often impressive, sometimes the more impressive the sound of the term, the less impressive the betting style — kind of an inverse proportion law. If you are interested in layout strategies by many other names, Chapter Twelve will have some choices for you.

Has ESP ever been employed successfully to beat roulette?

The *Rouge Et Noir* magazine (published out of New York and now long defunct) was a strong advocate of ESP in gambling. In fact, the book *Winning at Casino Games* by The Staff of *Rouge Et Noir* (1966) encourages people to develop their psychokinesis or PK ability (i.e., the ability to move objects with the mind) and their future clairvoyance or Psi (to see the future) as a means for getting an edge at the casinos. In roulette, they recommended attempting to "think" the ball into a given section of the wheel or look at the future to predict where it would land. They were absolutely certain that these powers existed in human beings. Here's a brief excerpt from the book:

> The field of Parapsychology has already identified and confirmed the existence of Extra-Sensory Perception and Psychokinesis. It has also made significant progress towards production of this phenomena on demand. Further advances in the study of the art should profoundly influence the gaming industry.
>
> The astute casino owner is already making use of the experimental results to increase the effective house percentage. Knowledgeable gamblers, on the other hand, are using Parapsychology results to negate the house advantage and to increase the frequency and size of their wins.
>
> It isn't necessary for the player to understand the theories associated with the field of Parapsychology to successfully make use of ESP and PK. He must merely be receptive and positive in his belief in the possible receipt of signals and the successful application of the Psi performance. . . . The player must also be careful to be fully aware of the psychological factors affecting ESP and PK. He should also limit his play to periods during which these factors are favorable.

I personally don't know anyone who can do this on a consistent basis. I actually don't know anyone who can do this at all. I also don't know of any casino that employs ESP as a management style. However, I have seen casino executives praying when a high roller is hitting a hot streak, so maybe prayer is in the management handbook. I do know that we all get hunches, have feelings about the future, and so on. Often these are correct. These we tend to remember. Often they are wrong. Those we tend to forget. Psychologist J.B. Rhine of Duke University did some controversial experiments in the 1950s and 1960s concerning the possible ability of the human mind to move objects or predict outcomes. He seemed to think it was possible based on his experiments. Critics of his experiments said he had confused statistical fluctuation for ESP. My advice? If it makes you feel good to try to think the ball into the pockets you're betting on, then think away! It can't hurt. (There's *Scobe's Wager* again.) Conversely, I would be somewhat leery if a small voice inside my head said: "Bet the ranch on number **17**."

What are the odds that every number will come up just once in 38 spins?

Hold your breath — or, rather, — don't hold your breath — because the odds of every number hitting just once in 38 spins are one in two quadrillion. With 5,000 roulette wheels going all day and all night, this will occur maybe once in 20 to 25 million years! So for those who like offering absurd proposition bets and can find a sucker who'll take them, try this: "I'll bet you (sucker) that all 38 numbers won't come up once each and I'll give you a $1,000 to one if they do. We'll do this as many times as you like (sucker) so let's get started."

You talk about biased wheels but what if the casino knows the wheel is biased and moves it around?

This has been a problem for wheel trackers in the past. If a casino knows one of its wheels is biased, it will move it to another location or *remove* it from the floor entirely. This is precisely what happened to Joseph Jaggers, the first biased-wheel player of note (circa 1873). He had been hammering Monte Carlo for days when an astute executive realized that there must be something wrong with the wheel that allowed this Jaggers to win. In the night, they moved the wheel. The next day Jaggers played his BIG Numbers on a non-biased wheel and was in turn hammered by the casino. However, Jaggers was no dope. As an engineer, he had a logical, methodical mind. He realized that the casino must have moved his wheel. What's more, he remembered that the wheel he had been playing had a slight mark on it. He toured the casino and, lo and behold, he once again located *his* wheel. He played and won again. Jaggers' experience should teach us that, as a standard procedure, the wheel tracker should make a note of any distinguishing characteristics on the wheel — type of wood, scratches, serial number, or the like. Thus, when you clock a wheel, don't just note the location but supply yourself with the most information possible about it. Then if or when the casino moves it, you'll be able to locate it. Of course, the casinos are often helped in discovering biased wheels by the wheel trackers themselves. Usually after the tracker wins a large amount of money over an extended period of time even the dullest pit person will realize something is wrong with the wheel. There's no way to stop this from happening but some techniques may help to prolong your stay at a wheel. Team play helps, for example. If members of a team alternate their playing time (never giving evidence that they recognize each other when they switch shifts), this can extend their life at a given wheel. Another technique is to camouflage your play by betting other, non-biased numbers near the hot number *on the layout.* Thus, if the hot number is two, you would bet one, two and three individually (with a somewhat bigger bet on two) or a line bet with two, or a column bet of the two column, or a dozens bet with the two. This style of betting makes it appear as if you are a regular player as opposed to a biased-wheel player. The downside of camouflage is that it costs you money since the other numbers are not biased, or worse, might be negatively biased since a number that is positively biased is stealing hits from other numbers. *The Biased Wheel Handbook* by Mark Billings and Brent Fredrickson has an interesting discussion of how to camouflage bets. Their thesis is that properly done, camouflaging reduces fluctuations and allows a player to hang in there longer. It's worth a look.

How can you really distinguish bias from random in short runs?

Technically, you can't. However, *Scobe's Wager* ("if it can't hurt you, you have nothing to lose in trying it") would apply long-range analysis and indicators to the short-range results. If you have a single biased number, or BIG Number, you might find that other numbers near it, or next to it, are getting fewer hits because the "biased" number is gobbling up the ball. If the sector itself is biased, you will notice that other numbers next to or near the BIG Number are also hitting with a greater frequency. Short runs, I must stipulate, are notoriously fickle. What appears to be a strong bias can vanish never to return. Still, it can't hurt to have some criteria for short term play, so why not these?

Have computers been used to beat roulette?

Yes. In a wonderful book, *The Eudaemonic Pie* (Vintage Books), Thomas A. Bass recounts his adventures with a computer in the casinos. In fact, Bass and Edward O. Thorp (the father of card counting in blackjack) both attempted to use computers to win at roulette. Thorp's attempt was more hypothetical (see Chapter Twelve), while Bass went into the jaws of the casino shark with his device and even pulled out some of the beast's teeth. The problem with all computer play is twofold: 1. being able to create a fully-functioning non-temperamental device that can analyze the spin of the ball, the velocity of the wheel, the likely reentry position of the ball, quickly enough to relay this information in usable form to a person just about to bet; and 2. actually doing this under casino conditions where the bets have to be made in the small time between the dealer's initial spinning of the ball and when he calls for "no more bets." There is a third problem, unfortunately. Most states now have laws against bringing electronic gaming devices (specifically computers) into casinos. For example, if you're caught with one of these things in Nevada, you face a 10-year prison sentence. The only roulette you'll find in the Nevada State Penitentiary is of the Russian variety. While it's fun to speculate about the devastation you could have wrought on the casino's bankroll with a handy-dandy pocket computer, the fact is you'll be fried in your own circuitry if you attempt to do so.

I enjoy playing Martingales. But I want to be able to extend the Martingale further than just eight steps. Any suggestions?

You must have a constitution of iron because by the ninth step of a Martingale, your wager is at table limit (if you can even get to this step). You can extend your Martingale by lowering the wagers on many of the steps. Instead of doubling bets, bet an equal amount as all your previous bets plus one (this is kind of a reverse Grand Martingale System). When you win, you will recoup all your losses plus one. Let's take a look at a typical table. The limits are $5 to $1,000. A regular Martingale would end at step 8 ($5, $10, $20, $40, $80, $160, $320, $640) since we would not be allowed to double $640. The total loss on that eighth step would be a staggering $1,275. If we wanted to get past the eighth step, here's how to do it: $5, $6, $12, $24, $48, $96, $192, $384, $768. This betting scheme gets us to nine steps. Keep in mind that at that ninth step we are betting $768 to win one dollar. My heart couldn't take that. Do you want to get to ten steps? Have a friend or partner place a second wager for the final amount on the layout. Just don't let the casino know that the two of you are pals. In a normal Martingale, we were stopped at $640 and needed to bet $1,280 to continue to step nine. So, you bet $1,000 and have someone else bet $280. You would do the same with our reverse Grand Martingale to get to ten. You bet $1,000 and have a buddy bet $536. Personally, I think you would have to be crazy to do any extended Martingale. But if you're going to go nuts, you might as well go all the way.

Of all the numbers on a roulette wheel, which number receives the most action?

According to all reports (all unofficial), the number that receives the most action, that is to say, the most popular number for straight-up betting purposes is number **17**. Perhaps it's because the number is in the middle of the layout (almost) or equidistant between *0* and *00* on the American double-zero wheel. Curiously, **17** is the number that actor Sean Connery supposedly bet and won on three consecutive spins at the casino in St. Vincent, Italy. He made $30,000 in that sequence. However, while the former James Bond, Connery, was making his killing in Italy, hundreds, if not thousands, of pathetic losers were emulating the real James Bond's betting scheme for roulette (from Ian Fleming's novels) which was simply to bet the first two dozens and those directly on the numbers. This strategy was employed by 007 in *Casino Royale* with astonishing results — Bond won five of six spins and made a hefty profit. Oh, well, in fiction Lady Luck is not controlling the outcomes, the author is. Had Fleming wanted, he could have had 007 hit a hundred times in a row. Still, one must pity the poor schnooks who went to the casinos, inspired by the debonair killer of spies and lover of women, and did the following: "My name is Schnook, *Poor* Schnook . . . give me a martini, shaken, not stirred, and put a $100 on each of the first 24 numbers straight up."

I remember once hearing a song about the man who broke the bank at Monte Carlo. Who was it? And how much did he win?

In Chapter One I mentioned that no one actually broke the bank of a casino but that *table banks* have been broken on occasion. This simply means that the table ran out of money. In today's casinos this would be the equivalent of a chip tray. Casinos can and do quickly replace the chips and continue to function when this happens. Even today, banks are occasionally broken throughout the world. At dice a hot hand can empty a table of chips. Interestingly enough, most tables stock more than enough chips for the anticipated action that the table will receive. It's only when big bettors are at a table and a hot streak occurs that the casino might lose the table bank. The song that you're referring to is "The Man Who Broke the Bank at Monte Carlo" and it does refer to a real gambler. His name was Charles Wells (born 1841, died 1926). It is estimated that he won close to a half million dollars at Monte Carlo on two trips in 1891. On the first trip he broke the table bank a dozen times. He was hot. On one 30-spin sequence, he won 23 times! After his first visit, the casino executives figured he was either a biased-wheel player or a cheat. They examined the wheel he had played and found that it was functioning normally. Then they interviewed the staff to see if there had been any collusion between them and him. Nothing. When Wells came back several months later, the casino had a small division of detectives watching his every move. Nothing helped. They could find no evidence of wrongdoing. And Wells hammered them again. That's when the song was written. What was Wells' secret? Pure, blind, dumb *luck*. He bet the numbers he felt would win and he guessed right. Evidently, he must have *felt* that he had inadvertently discovered some method of play and when he came back to Monte Carlo a third time in 1892 (in a huge yacht no less) with a fully worked-out, foolproof system of play, he lost everything he had won and then some. His luck had turned as soon as he employed his foolproof system and the man who broke the bank at Monte Carlo was himself broken. He died a desperate man. What lesson is to be learned from the man who broke the bank at Monte Carlo? That once they write a song about you, it's time to retire!

I'm concerned about the casinos cheating me at roulette. I remember that scene in Casablanca where the roulette wheel was fixed. Do you think the casinos would cheat at roulette? If so, how do they do it?

The scene you're referring to delineates Rick's (Humphrey Bogart's) character. He obviously has a good heart as he lets a hapless young man win his and his young bride's visas to the United States. Although Bogey's Rick is all sentiment and tender feelings, that doesn't stop him from having a gaffed wheel. In fact, gaffed wheels were often the norm in illegal casinos throughout the world and very few illegal casino operators have much sentiment and they eat tender feelings for breakfast. Darwin Ortiz, an expert in casino games and casino scams, has this to say in his excellent book, *Gambling Scams* (Carol Publishing), about cheating at roulette:

> A roulette wheel is composed of two major sections, the freely revolving center section which contains the num-

bered slots and the stationary outer wooden border on which the ball is spun which is called the backtrack. A casino operator who wants to take the gamble out of roulette will install four electromagnets at equidistant points inside the backtrack. He will also be sure to use a roulette ball that contains a steel core.

At the start of each play, the wheel is revolved counterclockwise and the ball is spun clockwise. As the wheel and the ball start to slow down, the operator will wait until the ball is directly above the segment of the wheel in which he wants it to land. He then turns on the juice for an instant. The pull of the magnets causes the ball to leave the track and start its descent to the numbered pockets.

Most operators . . . are not concerned with making a particular number win, but only with guaranteeing that certain numbers lose. All the operator has to do is to ensure that the ball falls in a section of the wheel far from the number that bears the largest bet. If the big money is either on odd or red, the operator sends the ball towards the zero. This slot is green and has an even black number on each side. Thus, if the ball lands in any of these three adjoining compartments the player will lose. If the big bettor wagers on even or black, the operator sends the ball toward the double zero, which is also green and has an odd red number on each side, again giving him three chances to beat the player.

As far as your fear of being cheated in a legitimate casino goes, I would forget it. Consider that the casinos are allowed to "rig" the game legally by not paying back the true odds and therefore it makes absolutely no sense for them to jeopardize their licenses by illegally rigging a game still more. However, if you continue to fear cheating, the next time you play observe the big player at the table for a few spins. If his action is heavy and he's losing, bet as far away from his numbers as possible. If he's betting even or odd, red or black, then follow Ortiz's description above and head for the green zero or double-zero with your bet!

While players really don't have much to fear from the casinos cheating them, the casinos have much more to fear from players attempting to cheat the casinos. The most common method of cheating the casinos at roulette is called *past posting.* Past posting is making a bet after the decision has already occurred. In roulette, a bettor quickly places a bet on the winning number or proposition as soon as the ball lands in the pocket. Betting in this fashion is a 100 percent guarantee of winning — if you don't get caught, that is. Past posting is probably the most popular form of cheating by players at casino games. Its unpopular counterpart is *bail posting* after getting caught!

How often does the ball hit the obstructions on its way towards the pockets?

I know of no study that discusses this. The obstructions have been placed to thwart visual wheel trackers from ascertaining where the ball will land. It also helps to thwart computer trackers. However, not all spins result in the ball hitting the obstructions and these are the spins that the visual trackers and computer trackers make their money on. Darwin Ortiz states that in 25 percent of the spins, the ball will go smoothly from the backtrack into the pockets. I did a little experiment in regard to this. I watched/recorded 500 spins. One hundred seven times the ball did not hit an obstruction. I don't know if this reflects the true average or not but it is not so far removed from Ortiz's estimate.

I have heard that sometimes biased wheels will remain on the floor of a casino for a long time. How can this be if people are winning money on it?

If the wheel is getting a lot of action, it is quite possible that the casino won't be aware that the wheel is biased because it is making a normal profit. If biased-wheel players play coolly and don't get too greedy, the casino will have no idea that the wheel has been analyzed and found out. Here's an extreme example to prove the point. Let us say that 38 bettors bet one dollar each on one number. Each player bets this same number 100 times. Only one number is biased, say, 12. It comes up 50 times. A biased wheel player is betting that number each time. Will the casino lose money? No. All the other numbers are being bet on every spin so the biased number is irrelevant to the casino's profits. Some number may not hit at all and that player will lose every bet. The casino becomes concerned when the biased number receives heavier action than all the other numbers because that's when the casino loses money.

10

Roulette by the Numbers

The following charts are composed of roulette decisions from actual wheels. They were not generated by computer, therefore they may not be fully random. It might be interesting to try some of the short-term wheel tracking techniques on some of these decisions. You might also find it interesting to play some of the layout strategies to see how far you'll get before the big loss occurs. The numbers in **bold** are black, the numbers in plain type are red, and the *italics* are green (*0* or *00*). All the decisions are from the American double-zero wheel. You'll note that all decisions are shown as scoreboards of 20 hits. All the decisions come from various electronic scoreboards in Atlantic City and Las Vegas. When a scoreboard only registered 16 numbers, we recorded four extra hits to bring the total to 20.

25	14	12	30	8	2	12
29	1	5	24	23	0	20
2	34	30	25	26	5	20
29	34	8	30	6	20	36
25	30	21	25	11	15	25
36	2	14	32	27	20	16
16	0	10	28	29	23	3
10	30	21	11	10	12	10
2	12	14	35	16	18	5
8	26	2	34	4	31	36
5	4	30	20	34	3	16
22	17	26	27	0	20	26
29	4	00	18	10	32	32
27	21	31	27	10	30	28
12	18	19	33	19	24	4
16	35	30	28	19	23	24
3	11	12	35	12	32	18
23	24	14	26	4	20	22
14	32	00	28	7	28	0
33	11	0	23	17	25	34

34	2	21	29	16	1	13
35	30	10	2	9	22	10
0	2	8	12	7	6	1
1	36	1	6	17	35	0
18	36	25	7	00	6	17
25	17	6	1	10	18	30
10	17	17	0	26	7	14
4	19	23	27	19	29	8
2	11	24	22	10	0	11
3	15	10	5	31	22	14
26	36	27	19	13	17	20
29	0	32	24	29	9	29
36	20	33	19	21	30	3
25	3	13	10	24	7	16
13	10	28	26	22	30	36
31	14	8	32	26	2	15
35	21	6	14	4	7	31
5	23	8	9	32	1	30
24	33	16	15	15	20	25
14	00	10	28	31	8	5

31	23	5	25	28	19	13
32	25	27	20	6	0	26
28	3	23	34	4	1	9
27	36	30	7	22	19	29
18	23	1	23	12	25	30
4	18	34	30	17	12	23
27	28	7	31	11	1	0
29	13	19	00	18	2	29
1	9	21	13	33	26	7
15	7	18	11	9	13	29
00	0	33	25	1	6	35
34	34	25	22	3	17	15
1	10	5	13	33	16	14
16	24	15	24	35	18	16
10	00	27	24	22	12	20
22	15	16	34	12	10	31
19	1	00	17	24	8	6
0	27	12	4	13	18	9
15	6	23	33	31	5	19
9	32	7	14	5	27	26

20	7	21	22	26	31	18
24	18	4	7	26	14	12
5	14	20	26	10	11	18
6	14	6	12	27	31	13
16	24	2	22	10	14	9
21	11	36	12	36	22	18
10	13	34	11	34	4	19
34	21	11	00	24	7	16
23	26	18	17	23	33	31
34	31	28	3	4	21	23
7	15	21	33	30	12	4
20	24	15	18	29	27	8
23	14	13	0	9	14	16
5	1	18	00	27	11	9
4	0	11	25	19	17	7
3	26	12	0	17	2	36
00	4	17	31	11	32	34
31	5	29	00	34	0	19
22	25	29	18	28	13	11
11	22	0	31	14	4	35

34	8	27	18	21	5	36
18	18	22	7	13	30	24
15	17	31	22	3	4	13
32	34	9	11	00	7	25
14	00	32	16	28	9	18
0	31	17	19	0	18	26
00	12	29	22	0	21	25
10	24	22	35	10	10	25
20	33	10	9	28	23	32
8	15	28	34	18	11	23
6	34	24	36	12	24	22
4	16	3	4	9	32	1
28	9	22	0	00	23	21
2	34	31	6	3	14	3
18	15	16	21	4	00	15
00	27	17	23	18	4	11
10	19	21	28	18	18	18
34	34	25	34	32	32	31
27	12	4	27	3	17	28
21	0	19	3	32	19	19

34	27	35	5	27	34	31
4	2	6	16	7	5	33
17	4	34	32	7	36	32
14	29	2	0	8	13	32
14	20	14	30	19	35	12
5	21	5	2	12	21	7
15	26	11	32	2	0	12
15	7	0	20	12	26	15
17	29	3	24	22	7	00
29	8	26	9	15	21	17
22	35	26	3	26	6	00
25	5	0	31	20	30	35
34	2	14	24	19	32	34
32	17	14	29	15	0	11
23	7	27	36	14	16	9
3	9	16	13	34	6	18
15	0	1	1	21	5	12
18	28	5	32	28	6	23
0	34	9	24	30	21	17
17	33	10	33	32	2	33

29	1	12	16	31	23	15
17	9	21	10	4	36	22
00	3	4	28	9	32	17
2	2	0	32	3	9	25
9	11	19	2	4	7	11
13	34	8	2	5	0	10
8	4	25	17	13	12	7
19	21	24	6	2	35	1
17	14	22	23	20	6	8
13	34	29	7	33	36	9
17	27	33	30	26	2	0
12	19	26	15	24	34	0
9	4	14	34	23	32	21
4	36	11	3	10	30	20
9	18	19	23	28	25	31
7	1	34	14	17	12	27
35	32	12	34	5	35	9
21	11	16	8	4	25	25
19	29	23	27	2	27	32
20	35	21	19	13	7	33
9	26	29	23	16	3	35
17	4	21	15	23	9	36
3	16	36	22	13	24	19
10	25	11	0	18	18	0
33	30	13	23	0	28	9
34	22	23	30	18	5	21
21	34	29	0	2	7	4
28	20	1	33	3	31	18
29	7	14	35	19	16	30
6	36	9	1	23	23	36
5	28	13	29	9	18	28
31	0	23	11	12	30	14
24	18	9	32	9	30	25
24	29	00	10	35	33	28
34	26	0	10	4	11	16
36	18	26	10	6	12	8
30	20	7	17	18	5	25
1	3	23	24	23	11	19
1	33	26	12	10	16	7
15	29	31	27	28	13	00

31	9	8	31	12	11	26
25	8	4	5	15	12	18
19	13	16	2	26	17	1
0	30	3	26	14	0	7
3	18	34	1	19	8	30
14	17	13	17	26	28	24
13	21	22	33	22	35	20
19	26	15	17	8	2	23
0	16	18	0	25	0	24
00	24	27	9	2	24	29
27	35	10	9	32	32	33
28	2	1	27	34	18	18
32	10	21	4	14	20	10
7	4	15	18	2	11	11
19	4	17	11	16	12	32
10	15	20	00	4	7	23
21	22	26	1	16	13	6
32	9	8	11	27	16	23
22	9	30	2	16	25	23
15	13	11	28	19	21	2

1	5	36	5	34	18	3
22	12	8	13	15	2	27
34	24	3	0	23	5	35
15	26	30	33	22	29	15
17	27	5	34	10	26	35
0	31	34	21	6	27	6
18	33	28	9	10	15	4
1	31	25	36	4	29	24
11	30	15	7	28	22	18
35	13	20	31	28	9	8
30	26	8	31	1	33	7
5	28	17	1	1	27	30
21	8	33	21	2	23	22
21	19	18	25	6	19	5
13	14	31	32	0	32	32
0	12	8	3	11	0	33
26	17	18	0	30	3	26
14	0	7	3	18	34	1
19	8	14	7	34	23	3
6	18	27	12	9	16	13

15	1	7	34	36	27	23
16	12	21	1	21	7	27
25	**11**	14	**24**	3	**31**	14
0	**29**	18	**17**	**22**	25	25
11	**4**	7	**29**	**26**	**35**	30
22	7	**22**	34	**17**	*0*	9
15	5	27	**22**	*0*	**2**	3
12	*0*	32	**11**	**24**	14	32
11	**20**	*0*	23	25	34	3
30	34	**26**	25	**11**	**15**	**22**
22	3	**29**	**8**	21	16	**31**
18	**2**	32	**22**	23	**2**	**29**
24	34	23	5	1	**28**	**20**
1	23	**31**	**24**	1	3	14
28	9	30	21	32	12	**22**
5	19	**29**	34	**26**	**15**	34
30	14	**17**	**13**	**17**	**26**	**24**
13	21	**22**	**35**	**22**	19	**26**
15	**17**	21	**4**	23	12	27
8	**2**	23	*00*	16	18	*0*

5	**28**	25	**35**	**15**	*0*	**2**
24	19	36	9	*0*	14	9
7	**15**	21	21	**22**	**22**	**33**
5	**35**	12	12	*0*	*00*	27
28	23	**22**	**11**	3	14	**33**
34	14	1	**11**	12	23	**33**
26	**15**	9	23	18	25	12
3	*0*	5	**10**	21	**24**	*00*
11	*0*	**13**	3	**10**	16	**10**
3	**31**	**15**	14	**31**	32	34
32	**2**	**10**	27	32	14	5
16	12	18	7	9	**17**	1
22	**33**	14	**28**	7	19	**10**
32	21	**33**	5	**24**	**2**	19
00	19	**31**	5	3	**31**	14
25	5	7	**31**	29	*0*	**29**
24	32	1	**2**	4	**26**	*0*
22	19	32	**2**	8	**8**	**2**
23	*00*	16	16	18	25	**8**
12	**4**	**6**	**24**	27	9	**2**

24	2	5	7	18	12	29
25	36	27	8	2	2	5
22	28	34	22	15	5	36
11	6	31	00	4	20	16
2	9	8	32	18	2	12
16	12	32	16	4	15	13
35	30	24	4	12	3	28
32	9	14	11	0	11	16
18	22	34	3	11	00	35
31	2	18	3	33	3	36
28	8	19	35	2	11	11
28	13	31	2	16	35	4
8	30	20	25	29	20	5
18	34	23	21	30	31	11
10	23	26	31	24	19	23
5	14	1	2	31	1	11
6	21	15	15	25	21	18
30	4	8	13	35	7	17
12	6	13	16	8	4	9
0	17	3	13	12	6	27
34	25	31	7	17	2	7
21	20	30	7	2	12	3
25	18	17	8	26	29	6
3	3	5	9	13	23	3
8	28	23	9	0	11	00
11	25	36	34	27	4	32
34	25	00	5	34	26	35
28	4	25	22	0	34	2
10	32	5	18	30	32	00
32	6	12	12	18	3	5
20	31	8	2	12	6	3
26	12	18	17	7	25	28
2	8	13	24	5	11	31
26	00	0	1	0	11	11
36	33	23	26	5	33	26
5	26	36	28	4	26	22
34	1	9	36	6	18	29
33	00	32	24	31	5	11
14	12	15	19	18	6	17
18	4	12	0	31	8	21

1	5	20	3	21	5	21
7	29	19	8	34	4	0
23	35	32	23	36	25	34
28	16	18	5	20	17	24
7	34	8	19	21	27	24
35	26	24	22	3	34	28
21	4	4	8	9	26	5
24	23	23	35	14	5	7
2	27	8	10	6	33	9
36	30	2	32	5	36	32
15	00	21	20	9	2	21
00	00	6	32	29	23	4
8	3	26	36	31	32	35
21	1	21	2	6	15	10
2	8	18	35	21	14	15
9	14	36	21	33	2	26
35	7	27	34	22	18	23
12	1	18	24	8	9	19
17	20	33	12	7	9	25
26	4	17	18	10	21	3

11	4	7	23	8	34	32
17	31	35	36	4	16	12
28	13	16	32	8	2	5
16	19	27	28	19	8	27
8	8	31	17	35	30	14
23	27	22	1	18	27	8
34	31	26	18	6	10	11
3	00	30	8	30	32	2
30	12	30	7	24	21	8
0	28	13	20	16	1	12
16	10	33	11	8	17	23
21	8	0	28	21	13	29
20	16	1	2	10	33	11
8	17	30	23	7	25	22
0	33	29	33	3	6	7
9	00	27	00	4	35	25
31	35	16	15	32	13	13
24	30	11	8	9	32	16
3	33	21	6	15	25	2
16	10	26	16	9	8	26

20	3	5	18	31	9	34
4	4	24	7	9	16	19
20	15	18	36	7	9	7
5	10	0	33	14	7	13
25	35	1	12	24	19	1
9	8	29	24	36	29	0
24	36	12	2	17	23	9
3	4	20	19	18	11	2
10	00	11	5	33	29	32
22	29	31	15	17	16	13
21	21	00	31	0	20	3
1	00	32	15	2	1	2
30	33	35	16	00	11	25
15	32	23	30	5	14	27
5	2	5	5	17	16	3
33	21	6	15	25	2	16
10	26	16	9	8	26	20
3	5	18	31	9	20	15
18	36	7	9	7	7	5
10	0	33	14	7	13	25

35	1	12	24	19	1	9
8	29	24	36	29	0	24
36	27	2	19	4	23	15
26	34	30	21	00	14	33
17	16	27	35	36	00	9
3	32	29	17	12	15	28
33	2	3	36	12	34	2
1	1	32	28	4	3	8
23	5	26	24	11	19	33
35	32	27	24	18	24	28
19	6	20	31	19	19	28
7	2	0	0	13	19	4
30	21	00	33	19	13	29
26	16	3	31	4	9	25
20	0	00	30	16	33	28
17	24	24	34	32	11	15
36	4	1	35	1	29	33
26	00	18	31	18	28	36
8	29	36	29	30	1	13
9	32	26	34	8	00	1

21	30	**33**	**35**	9	**6**	21
30	7	7	**26**	**15**	**29**	23
31	**15**	**28**	8	**20**	**11**	**11**
27	14	3	**2**	18	21	**11**
36	**26**	**4**	**26**	34	**13**	32
26	**4**	**17**	5	**22**	**22**	**17**
00	16	14	**6**	**31**	**33**	*00*
21	**2**	3	**10**	27	12	19
35	**24**	27	**29**	**11**	**17**	32
00	**31**	1	**22**	23	**11**	27
24	**35**	**28**	**33**	3	36	5
27	**2**	12	23	*0*	*0*	3
8	27	**24**	12	**20**	**35**	*0*
14	**6**	5	25	**17**	21	27
11	**24**	34	**33**	34	3	23
1	**10**	**11**	14	**10**	**13**	**35**
33	14	*0*	**6**	**4**	25	21
36	**26**	18	5	**8**	3	23
14	**22**	21	36	**22**	**33**	14
10	**31**	16	19	**33**	23	16
23	1	1	14	**10**	**26**	25
0	30	**15**	32	27	14	14
3	*00*	16	25	*0*	27	34
29	**10**	19	**33**	**20**	**35**	30
4	*0*	14	1	21	**28**	32
25	**24**	**2**	12	1	25	**4**
10	**35**	**20**	**11**	**15**	**29**	**8**
14	**15**	9	**29**	**8**	3	32
20	25	**29**	**20**	**20**	**33**	36
12	*0*	23	**20**	**17**	18	30
34	3	*00*	16	25	*00*	**17**
1	**15**	34	**29**	12	*0*	34
34	32	*0*	23	**20**	9	19
1	**15**	**35**	36	30	25	12
11	**17**	16	14	**26**	**29**	**28**
21	**17**	5	**8**	**2**	1	*0*
31	*0*	16	34	**29**	27	**28**
29	**11**	14	**15**	1	*00*	**4**
0	**17**	**15**	*0*	23	5	21
15	12	**11**	**13**	1	**33**	**2**

0	00	4	4	35	0	6
14	11	31	27	20	22	35
0	26	23	36	1	7	26
16	36	29	22	16	8	18
1	6	14	13	14	35	18
28	7	17	32	31	3	2
3	27	3	14	33	14	1
34	13	18	9	00	1	12
10	11	35	24	34	7	30
3	21	30	9	22	23	16
22	15	2	8	31	11	31
26	16	34	2	1	26	00
7	5	30	6	36	5	3
23	2	14	27	29	10	13
28	24	7	4	12	2	6
2	17	21	31	13	9	35
32	1	6	31	7	1	28
28	29	21	18	36	8	19
10	1	23	2	32	9	19
5	17	29	30	36	21	19

4	34	13	32	22	19	22
1	8	6	30	2	13	31
3	33	16	15	35	30	0
5	19	25	29	19	11	11
17	35	36	31	26	2	26
4	2	27	1	5	00	35
28	5	32	2	29	7	23
35	6	7	3	28	1	35
23	14	3	11	1	7	5
12	36	11	7	5	30	20
4	4	7	33	34	26	23
14	15	33	4	3	5	23
30	3	20	23	0	30	10
21	5	4	9	14	30	21
20	26	00	28	12	11	35
22	2	33	30	12	1	12
14	24	0	27	30	12	20
24	6	25	6	27	5	13
18	8	35	12	32	15	5
13	5	8	9	33	34	31

36	**15**	1	**10**	18	**20**	5
25	14	7	9	27	**28**	3
17	12	**31**	**24**	3	23	19
21	1	**13**	*00*	**20**	19	18
30	**22**	**26**	**22**	**26**	**4**	30
2	*0*	34	30	**20**	**22**	1
27	**2**	30	23	18	**26**	**15**
18	**4**	**10**	**28**	*0*	19	7
11	32	14	19	**11**	*00*	**17**
33	12	**11**	**26**	23	**6**	**26**
28	25	25	*0*	32	36	**15**
3	**33**	7	**28**	**11**	30	36
28	*00*	32	1	16	**22**	16
4	*0*	9	25	*0*	7	**28**
18	25	**13**	19	**29**	35	35
10	**17**	18	**22**	32	*0*	35
5	36	**24**	21	**11**	**13**	3
4	14	19	**8**	**11**	**2**	**4**
35	**28**	23	9	**31**	**28**	**31**
14	**26**	**22**	**4**	34	27	5
8	**10**	**6**	**20**	**29**	**6**	**13**
00	**29**	**17**	**35**	12	12	**26**
13	**11**	1	*0*	**11**	**10**	**4**
30	**6**	**4**	*00*	**4**	27	**28**
27	**2**	3	18	16	**31**	**17**
3	**24**	23	34	3	**26**	**8**
3	**2**	32	7	*0*	9	**33**
11	**8**	*00*	**4**	**31**	**8**	**20**
1	**11**	1	19	34	12	16
21	**8**	7	36	**15**	**35**	1
27	18	**17**	**17**	34	**24**	9
4	32	21	**2**	16	**17**	**15**
2	*00*	12	**31**	**22**	30	**20**
17	**24**	**4**	21	**8**	18	23
6	**4**	36	1	**8**	**28**	9
8	9	19	12	*00*	**26**	1
34	9	**20**	1	21	7	21
34	**15**	16	*0*	32	**20**	**15**
27	14	32	**35**	**8**	30	1
32	36	**22**	**31**	18	**22**	**10**

31	32	**28**	**35**	**26**	**28**	**26**
20	9	**33**	12	**31**	25	**35**
30	3	**8**	**13**	19	**26**	**4**
30	**35**	**11**	**13**	25	21	12
19	12	21	*0*	**13**	3	**6**
00	**10**	**31**	**4**	**10**	24	**10**
1	**28**	7	**10**	**31**	30	**10**
30	7	1	27	5	32	19
35	23	30	*00*	**35**	12	**13**
00	**15**	**11**	**8**	**24**	21	**4**
28	**17**	5	3	30	**35**	**24**
30	7	1	5	**31**	**13**	**4**
25	7	9	**2**	**22**	3	**29**
17	32	23	**2**	**24**	3	**13**
29	**26**	**20**	19	*0*	36	12
23	21	5	**35**	**33**	3	5
33	**17**	**29**	**31**	**11**	**35**	3
28	9	**17**	23	**8**	9	**22**
2	**22**	**13**	**20**	**8**	**13**	*00*
11	12	**11**	21	18	1	12

2	30	16	32	**33**	36	1
21	**35**	3	**28**	9	**17**	23
8	9	**22**	**2**	**22**	**13**	**20**
8	**13**	*00*	12	**11**	21	18
1	12	**2**	30	16	23	32
33	**33**	**28**	21	**6**	**35**	16
7	16	**6**	7	**20**	5	12
25	**11**	5	19	**20**	**17**	**15**
9	14	**31**	**28**	36	34	**2**
24	5	25	14	23	**17**	*00*
17	**6**	**10**	**33**	**35**	36	25
1	**8**	32	*0*	**20**	**24**	7
11	**6**	12	25	5	30	**2**
17	12	5	14	**8**	9	27
9	**20**	**13**	*0*	14	32	**4**
29	**24**	18	3536	18	**17**	
7	**2**	1	7	**35**	**13**	*00*
35	25	**10**	**8**	**22**	23	7
25	**26**	**4**	**35**	16	12	32
8	5	**22**	14	**31**	**35**	**2**

19	34	**17**	**4**	**11**	30	**11**
7	**22**	12	30	**29**	3	**29**
32	34	**4**	18	3	23	**15**
30	*00*	**20**	5	9	**15**	7
8	**29**	30	**4**	5	**2**	**15**
12	27	36	**24**	34	12	**29**
10	*0*	3	**8**	3	**13**	**22**
20	**26**	**10**	19	**29**	23	**22**
1	25	**33**	**22**	7	**28**	16
3	**15**	**31**	**11**	3	18	**35**
6	**33**	**28**	32	32	*0*	34
21	**17**	**33**	14	**10**	18	**28**
16	**6**	7	21	23	*0*	19
17	**6**	14	23	**17**	25	*00*
36	**26**	36	12	**15**	21	19
18	**20**	1	**29**	12	1	**22**
4	**33**	18	27	30	7	27
33	**35**	3	**20**	**2**	12	**4**
34	**26**	**24**	21	**22**	16	18
24	36	**29**	**2**	**4**	16	3
1	*0*	**6**	21	**31**	23	5
30	9	**31**	**28**	**20**	34	36
7	**6**	**26**	27	**31**	32	34
4	34	**20**	25	**28**	**15**	**24**
1	*00*	23	25	25	**33**	36
3	**22**	**24**	34	16	1	**22**
11	**10**	*00*	**28**	7	25	**20**
30	**6**	**8**	*00*	**17**	12	**33**
21	32	*0*	**13**	**13**	**11**	14
27	**10**	25	7	7	**24**	27
30	**35**	19	5	**11**	**17**	7
17	16	12	14	27	**6**	**24**
33	19	**24**	**22**	**35**	16	**24**
11	30	3	36	36	**2**	19
12	**6**	**22**	**17**	9	14	7
30	14	**20**	12	**13**	12	30
16	**10**	**29**	34	19	27	9
22	1	**4**	**15**	**22**	*0*	21
17	**24**	**2**	**17**	**15**	7	16
19	**29**	**10**	**6**	**22**	**11**	**2**

5	16	*0*	5	27	12	*0*
13	**33**	34	25	**33**	14	5
7	16	**17**	18	5	18	**6**
19	**13**	**2**	**20**	**26**	**28**	27
9	**6**	**29**	24	13	5	9
00	**28**	**31**	13	**2**	**35**	**10**
2	**29**	**6**	16	**28**	16	9
13	**4**	**13**	34	3	16	7
00	*0*	**11**	3	**24**	**13**	**10**
00	19	5	21	32	9	14
18	*00*	**17**	**4**	9	**13**	**17**
2	**6**	**4**	21	**15**	23	**28**
1	25	**26**	21	**6**	**8**	23
6	**8**	27	**4**	36	32	1
36	**31**	**26**	23	**35**	3	**8**
11	16	**15**	23	**26**	**35**	36
4	25	25	14	25	36	9
1	**2**	**29**	**2**	**35**	**8**	**2**
6	**22**	**11**	**20**	**22**	19	*0*
1	5	**31**	**6**	**28**	**17**	18

12	**22**	*00*	**6**	**2**	1	**28**
36	7	**26**	23	16	32	9
4	**17**		**10**	*0*	**35**	3
3	**26**	**4**	7	32	19	**13**
16	25	12	19	14	23	**11**
25	**29**	36	18	**2**	**29**	**35**
2	14	32	**22**	**24**	**28**	**11**
26	27	36	23	27	32	**4**
5	**11**	9	18	**20**	16	14
33	25	7	**24**	19	**22**	34
15	1	1	**22**	32	**15**	**26**
12	5	**2**	**4**	25	**35**	21
3	16	**22**	12	**20**	**2**	32
8	12	**6**	**17**	**31**	**28**	23
15	**17**	**35**	14	**13**	25	27
18	**33**	32	**20**	1	36	21
34	36	**10**	**35**	**2**	**15**	23
2	14	1	**8**	7	16	14
35	**33**	**28**	**2**	9	**22**	34
0	1	**33**	12	**22**	**8**	1

6	9	12	**8**	**17**	6	**15**
31	**24**	9	16	14	6	**2**
34	**6**	*00*	**15**	**26**	23	**26**
18	**31**	**17**	**24**	**31**	**33**	32
00	*00*	32	**15**	**13**	30	1
4	**33**	**31**	32	30	30	32
2	**2**	25	**10**	**6**	**26**	36
00	**4**	**17**	3	25	21	**13**
9	*00*	30	**20**	25	**2**	**10**
18	**8**	9	**24**	30	12	**4**
19	**13**	**29**	30	19	9	**20**
4	**15**	12	*0*	1	18	*0*
2	*00*	**35**	**22**	30	**35**	27
3	25	**10**	**31**	21	14	**2**
35	21	14	21	**13**	9	**4**
35	16	19	**11**	27	**10**	25
11	25	14	**17**	*00*	**2**	9
0	**11**	**4**	9	16	**28**	21
15	34	12	30	36	**28**	**31**
5	**15**	**6**	30	**33**	*0*	**28**
24	**13**	**28**	23	*0*	25	**2**
26	25	**11**	14	**17**	*00*	**2**
19	*00*	**11**	14	19	**6**	**28**
21	**15**	34	12	30	36	**28**
31	5	**15**	**6**	30	**33**	*0*
28	14	23	27	23	*0*	**26**
13	18	**11**	18	**15**	**35**	9
4	**2**	**6**	**29**	32	32	*00*
0	32	**28**	18	9	18	23
6	3	25	**26**	**2**	**29**	5
30	**33**	**11**	14	34	16	32
25	**31**	9	**2**	9	1	**31**
1	**11**	**24**	*0*	25	12	9
0	34	*0*	5	**2**	1	**29**
12	**35**	5	**31**	**4**	19	18
22	18	**13**	14	**11**	**28**	3
2	**29**	19	**11**	**6**	21	16
18	**26**	12	12	**31**	**2**	1
14	27	19	**35**	**20**	9	1
25	**24**	**17**	**26**	23	4	**17**

19	12	21	**8**	7	3	25
31	**15**	1	19	32	**17**	16
26	19	**31**	30	**31**	12	14
3	**6**	25	**10**	**33**	1	**20**
10	**33**	16	3	**26**	5	27
36	**11**	*0*	19	7	7	*0*
6	**22**	36	**28**	16	**11**	19
4	**22**	24	13	**4**	3	5
34	**35**	20	**4**	5	**35**	**6**
8	**26**	3	**4**	**4**	36	**24**
3	18	**17**	13	7	**4**	32
32	34	**31**	**33**	30	12	**4**
3	25	**6**	16	34	**33**	16
8	25	**15**	27	36	7	*0*
8	25	30	30	23	**13**	*0*
11	36	**2**	**13**	14	21	14
28	**15**	18	**24**	**17**	23	32
23	*0*	**22**	**28**	9	**15**	25
16	*00*	**2**	**17**	5	27	12
34	**13**	**2**	16	**4**	**17**	**22**

11	**22**	**22**	**4**	12	**33**	19
3	**6**	1	34	1	*0*	18
9	**33**	36	**4**	14	21	1
5	**2**	34	**6**	**4**	18	16
10	*0*	12	**13**	24	3	**22**
8	**15**	1	23	18	**15**	23
25	16	32	7	3	**11**	20
17	*00*	32	*00*	**10**	21	**24**
24	34	**28**	19	3	**29**	7
13	**35**	18	1	**22**	25	**6**
33	12	30	5	**29**	9	3
15	12	**11**	30	1	**15**	36
30	**15**	**11**	*00*	3	12	9
3	12	1	**11**	23	12	**17**
9	**20**	18	*00*	1	36	32
27	23	*0*	**22**	14	**26**	20
28	**20**	**28**	5	**33**	34	**20**
24	**28**	*0*	**2**	23	**2**	**15**
24	**29**	25	16	23	3	**6**
20	**15**	34	**2**	18	**28**	**8**

26	11	10	26	17	28	21
17	28	16	7	29	15	18
16	31	9	2	30	28	15
6	7	15	14	11	7	23
11	12	1	13	26	11	11
26	20	8	31	6	2	4
22	6	8	15	4	30	3
7	1	20	5	12	13	20
3	14	13	2	4	00	2
14	35	1	23	12	1	1
27	32	0	26	8	35	32
17	5	20	29	19	16	4
0	19	12	23	5	26	10
22	0	0	8	34	9	23
34	32	20	32	8	19	21
17	5	15	29	30	13	18
13	35	20	16	17	2	4
17	00	26	33	35	1	20
3	28	19	34	9	8	10
00	3	33	32	32	29	00

2	6	15	1	0	18	11
31	26	0	11	13	25	00
8	4	3	26	28	21	15
6	2	8	27	5	14	0
29	14	33	27	27	6	18
1	14	21	34	32	33	32
4	20	4	29	2	34	27
18	21	1	16	8	21	12
32	20	19	5	19	34	1
24	19	21	26	00	18	36
18	15	9	32	13	31	0
25	11	20	24	30	17	23
22	6	24	14	14	18	0
31	24	28	15	36	4	13
23	8	19	2	32	22	5
9	6	15	22	23	2	9
4	24	23	33	28	25	0
36	10	27	34	00	10	11
30	25	34	4	0	9	33
1	10	17	12	17	10	1

24	16	**15**	**35**	9	**17**	3
29	**11**	23	**2**	18	**11**	**2**
6	36	**33**	1	34	18	23
11	**31**	**2**	12	1	3	9
36	23	27	**22**	36	12	**20**
14	34	*0*	**10**	**24**	1	1
11	16	**24**	32	**6**	5	25
3	**4**	36	**26**	24	**6**	**10**
31	1	3	25	**10**	**24**	*00*
6	30	**10**	25	*00*	21	32
24	32	**11**	9	34	**24**	**11**
34	**20**	5	**15**	1	**28**	**22**
27	23	**33**	**11**	21	**22**	12
14	30	**20**	**2**	30	**20**	**24**
24	27	**10**	32	**6**	**10**	**15**
13	32	**29**	3	**26**	5	7
29	**26**	18	14	**26**	**33**	3
3	**22**	32	27	**33**	3	**6**
9	30	**22**	**13**	8	18	**10**
31	7	*00*	**11**	19	**8**	**28**

23	**2**	**31**	**20**	3	**31**	**17**
16	**22**	9	5	*00*	*0*	**28**
26	**20**	3	**28**	**26**	**22**	**31**
27	**6**	**4**	36	*00*	27	7
11	*0*	**8**	**20**	23	3	**28**
32	7	**24**	**11**	9	**4**	14
12	30	**6**	16	21	**2**	34
35	23	32	21	21	25	**31**
10	**6**	**17**	19	5	*0*	**29**
26	25	**11**	**17**	7	**17**	14
1	**4**	18	**28**	3	**31**	32
4	5	**29**	1	9	34	**6**
1	3	**10**	**11**	32	**6**	**31**
13	**22**	*0*	9	*0*	12	16
34	**4**	**2**	**2**	*0*	**31**	**4**
0	16	32	12	**29**	7	5
29	30	**22**	9	9	**10**	32
29	7	**31**	3	**6**	25	**33**
31	21	*0*	**13**	**31**	**6**	**8**
6	3	**2**	1	**6**	34	3

00	18	6	2	15	25	24
35	21	4	17	16	35	35
28	35	5	29	31	15	26
36	35	9	11	7	6	20
11	1	11	23	6	12	31
5	4	13	14	5	20	3
12	23	29	36	8	14	34
22	2	1	6	34	17	35
0	0	33	23	12	36	26
31	5	20	0	24	4	9
3	31	0	17	32	22	23
22	13	1	16	10	15	18
30	32	10	29	27	3	33
3	1	30	8	00	16	15
33	18	24	35	21	1	5
19	19	21	29	33	29	14
34	23	9	20	4	7	1
35	3	36	19	0	19	9
6	4	22	34	4	1	9
1	9	4	32	35	12	33
11	28	25	0	29	15	1
25	23	25	15	33	12	29
33	27	19	1	11	0	6
9	12	0	16	12	16	18
17	13	14	4	12	28	17
24	0	0	20	32	23	3
23	24	28	3	32	7	16
35	17	33	14	36	1	19
28	8	25	9	0	4	12
11	8	0	00	33	22	13
7	17	11	29	13	29	36
34	5	8	7	9	12	4
29	22	15	34	25	28	35
0	30	4	31	20	7	31
00	5	8	29	14	35	1
0	18	18	0	24	2	28
23	18	31	6	11	6	31
2	4	14	34	6	36	9
5	31	13	29	31	20	16
33	14	16	23	6	3	18

30	23	**20**	**24**	1	**2**	**10**
19	5	12	**29**	**6**	**33**	**22**
17	9	**29**	16	*0*	5	**17**
31	30	16	**24**	**6**	**4**	**17**
35	*0*	23	**26**	**11**	**22**	**2**
8	**26**	34	**22**	12	19	**4**
23	**13**	32	3	**15**	*00*	16
5	**31**	**24**	27	23	30	7
30	**15**	**26**	36	**11**	36	**4**
36	18	14	**17**	19	**11**	**35**
28	23	**24**	**31**	25	**11**	**28**
29	**22**	14	**11**	**4**	18	32
1	**26**	25	18	16	**35**	**6**
27	*00*	*0*	**28**	21	**28**	*00*
5	**13**	**11**	9	36	**13**	34
18	12	**2**	**13**	36	34	**15**
25	**6**	1	25	**2**	**24**	23
4	27	**20**	**6**	21	36	**15**
30	**20**	19	12	**22**	**10**	21
23	16	**17**	21	**24**	**15**	**11**

33	**24**	7	5	32	**4**	27
9	18	9	**31**	27	3	**26**
21	27	**11**	32	**24**	30	14
10	27	**13**	34	3	**4**	**24**
30	**20**	12	5	12	**2**	**4**
14	5	**28**	27	*00*	**29**	19
13	21	7	**17**	1	**22**	25
28	**26**	12	14	18	18	**4**
15	27	1	16	**15**	14	**28**
5	*00*	**26**	30	**33**	**6**	25
24	**15**	**35**	**4**	**24**	**28**	**6**
24	**29**	3	30	**24**	**13**	32
8	3	14	**10**	25	**2**	34
4	*00*	3	34	**22**	**11**	**28**
3	23	*0*	**15**	14	19	32
8	34	**10**	27	**33**	19	**13**
00	27	19	**8**	*0*	5	36
13	**24**	30	9	25	**35**	23
30	14	34	**15**	**10**	30	3
28	**13**	**31**	**6**	**33**	30	34

5	1	9	*0*	**11**	9	1
4	7	9	18	*00*	**17**	**26**
19	27	**6**	**26**	16	30	**24**
0	**26**	**33**	3	**24**	**17**	14
7	**24**	**22**	*0*	**22**	5	**6**
20	**35**	5	**13**	19	**11**	18
14	3	**17**	*00*	**17**	**26**	9
25	**24**	12	**8**	25	19	18
18	1	12	**13**	**6**	23	18
27	**8**	**31**	36	*00*	23	12
29	7	**35**	16	*0*	**17**	12
6	21	**17**	**26**	32	**26**	**24**
30	12	27	7	**28**	25	19
16	12	**15**	**22**	**13**	**6**	3
18	**31**	**28**	**26**	*00*	**17**	34
30	1	34	36	**29**	**2**	**11**
24	12	**33**	**29**	**24**	*00*	**35**
25	**10**	**28**	**20**	9	1	16
4	3	3	**33**	**28**	**29**	**26**
20	30	**26**	*0*	**24**	1	12
9	36	27	21	18	12	18
13	**10**	7	18	**20**	**17**	36
1	**6**	19	**26**	**24**	27	9
11	**4**	**2**	*00*	5	9	**33**
17	12	**6**	**4**	7	**17**	16
35	**31**	**11**	**20**	21	19	19
3	**29**	**4**	19	**17**	12	**33**
1	5	**26**	25	1	**13**	**22**
15	**15**	7	36	**31**	**29**	27
22	12	14	12	18	**11**	19
21	23	12	9	**6**	1	**13**
20	34	23	34	1	*00*	14
3	16	23	**24**	**2**	1	**10**
7	14	**8**	**31**	**28**	30	**28**
22	27	23	1	**31**	7	**10**
10	**13**	**4**	**4**	9	25	**11**
26	**31**	**4**	*0*	*00*	9	*00*
14	**4**	32	34	32	**31**	7
6	16	**22**	19	**31**	12	14
17	5	7	14	32	**35**	9

6	18	23	9	21	6	9
11	2	1	0	13	36	36
0	0	5	11	18	24	9
31	16	19	15	29	30	13
36	26	36	0	5	31	1
35	15	32	00	25	2	11
26	2	18	7	2	24	4
6	7	5	21	14	28	20
10	16	36	29	3	18	30
26	1	6	18	17	7	8
3	5	20	36	26	32	26
7	2	7	16	2	17	16
25	36	17	30	6	3	36
17	17	14	15	27	17	3
4	23	27	36	15	27	00
5	7	10	31	17	12	9
12	19	2	4	2	17	20
14	27	00	8	5	36	11
12	11	31	3	23	17	14
13	5	33	22	7	11	32

33	10	30	23	7	16	12
16	30	30	16	5	13	3
0	4	8	5	9	23	20
10	26	29	12	3	16	8
17	29	36	10	23	11	26
27	36	24	16	30	18	22
18	30	0	34	26	18	3
8	25	36	11	3	32	33
17	0	24	22	11	1	25
00	20	9	30	0	20	28
26	22	34	20	21	33	27
25	00	0	29	7	11	9
17	27	7	8	25	18	18
19	32	8	22	33	28	3
34	26	36	28	34	28	30
24	13	18	6	36	29	10
10	9	23	12	10	14	36
0	36	25	4	2	22	8
27	29	30	33	7	14	16
5	9	20	20	0	25	31

34	16	**28**	16	**22**	16	*00*
00	**2**	**22**	**15**	25	**2**	18
12	**35**	3	12	18	27	*00*
9	**33**	19	**31**	25	*0*	**26**
27	**29**	**15**	**28**	21	**31**	**20**
30	5	12	1	**6**	19	1
34	7	1	**13**	**20**	*00*	**31**
5	34	14	**28**	**8**	5	*00*
0	*0*	14	27	5	19	12
4	**31**	**35**	21	**28**	*0*	**6**
9	**26**	18	**13**	**4**	**2**	**15**
15	3	21	**22**	21	9	7
30	**35**	34	30	5	1	**35**
20	**22**	*0*	**8**	**31**	16	**2**
33	**17**	**6**	21	23	**20**	**4**
22	23	**26**	5	**8**	5	5
00	3	14	**35**	30	**11**	**28**
26	**10**	23	*00*	**33**	**15**	25
20	18	19	21	**33**	**2**	**29**
3	25	1	18	**2**	**15**	**24**
00	**33**	**24**	9	*0*	**24**	**11**
8	23	*0*	**11**	**26**	**11**	**8**
0	1	**28**	*0*	36	27	**17**
22	16	**26**	5	30	9	18
7	**24**	**22**	*00*	**20**	**4**	18
20	19	**10**	5	14	**33**	**4**
24	**13**	7	19	**10**	30	**35**
19	36	18	**24**	18	34	**22**
2	**28**	36	27	1	**33**	36
4	16	5	21	3	23	**24**
31	**31**	**15**	**29**	1	36	**22**
5	34	21	21	25	3	16
32	**2**	**28**	18	12	**8**	23
32	5	14	**22**	27	19	1
12	**4**	**35**	**28**	**35**	**28**	21
15	1	19	**31**	**22**	*00*	23
7	**26**	**20**	25	**13**	19	9
25	5	16	32	3	7	7
19	**17**	32	27	**11**	**35**	**29**
5	34	**17**	9	**6**	*00*	32

6	1	29	19	22	22	36
25	21	24	29	30	5	28
24	26	14	20	18	2	14
35	1	12	22	19	19	4
35	9	29	7	11	15	8
11	20	24	14	29	8	35
23	20	33	20	28	00	15
24	22	2	32	25	3	22
8	13	3	18	12	0	10
27	22	12	2	33	30	26
19	26	0	10	19	15	33
18	14	23	35	17	34	31
23	2	34	9	12	2	12
31	20	7	23	25	26	00
21	28	10	0	6	5	00
34	34	11	25	24	32	17
18	00	22	11	21	18	17
8	30	24	21	29	2	26
32	10	1	10	22	36	15
9	16	0	00	23	19	7
28	00	0	28	34	7	8
29	13	2	15	28	24	11
28	0	00	26	7	21	9
1	9	33	36	5	22	16
11	4	0	27	18	7	35
23	7	3	13	31	1	16
10	18	32	19	16	6	24
23	30	27	33	27	27	33
32	36	23	13	15	27	24
22	35	29	20	30	10	24
12	12	19	20	13	14	24
26	23	15	13	00	3	21
25	0	3	13	33	7	8
21	4	20	29	13	9	18
11	1	25	11	28	13	36
11	23	29	24	35	33	20
30	3	28	6	34	00	2
32	13	26	35	26	36	5
8	21	34	31	23	36	18
35	18	35	7	7	9	0

0	12	**10**	*0*	**2**	**20**	5
5	25	21	34	**26**	21	**20**
13	27	**20**	34	**10**	**26**	21
14	34	**17**	5	**35**	**8**	21
00	**10**	**22**	36	**29**	27	3
14	**2**	9	**33**	*0*	21	**4**
19	**4**	9	25	**29**	**10**	18
0	**4**	**15**	**15**	16	1	**24**
29	25	19	**22**	18	**8**	30
19	19	**4**	3	**2**	**10**	**13**
28	**15**	**11**	**29**	**20**	**15**	9
16	27	7	21	32	**2**	25
20	5	7	5	**11**	16	**15**
25	16	30	**26**	*0*	**22**	7
30	9	30	**8**	**4**	21	**10**
18	30	*0*	9	**31**	32	**24**
22	**8**	34	**28**	**8**	**2**	**11**
14	**17**	18	**29**	27	**2**	*00*
10	**15**	**13**	**10**	**33**	**29**	32
23	12	**6**	19	**26**	**15**	19

11

Numbers from the Same Wheel

The following 3,800 numbers were all recorded from the same roulette wheel in a little less than a week of play. They were recorded by three of my researchers who were gallant enough, tireless enough, and, yes, *insane* enough to stand (or sit) at the table recording spin after spin after spin. This particular wheel did not have a scoreboard as I wanted a relatively older wheel (better chance of being biased). Most of the spins were continuous as the wheel was usually open both night and day and my researchers, Wayne, Gary and Heidi, kept continuous watch. When no one was playing the wheel, each individual would often play for small stakes to continue getting the numbers down.

There are some gaps, however, because of times when no one was watching the wheel. Wayne missed about a half an hour due to "too much grease at dinner." Heidi lost some time when she had an unplanned visit from Mother Nature reminding her that she was, indeed, still fertile and quite capable of playing genetic roulette should she desire another child at age 48.

Gary never missed a minute. ("Let your readers know I never missed a second.") Sorry. Gary never missed a *second.*

Still, these recording gaps were few and far between, and if the particular wheel recorded here is indeed biased (as I believe it is), it should have no real influence on any analysis you would like to do. I have split up the numbers into 10 groups of 380 spins each. Think of each group as a session of play. You read the numbers from top to bottom, then go to the top again. At a page break, the numbers from the last column continue on the first column of the next page. At the end of each group I have tallied the totals for all the major bets: hits for all the individual numbers, the dozens, the columns, red-black, odd-even and high-low. At the end of the 3,800 decisions, I have listed each number's appearance in a chart so you can see how that number fared in the course of play from one session to another in comparison to other numbers. I have totaled all the other bets as well. Also at the end, I have included the major streaks of even-money wagers that occured. Finally, in my comments section, I have given my slant on this wheel which I think shows an exploitable bias. All credit goes to Wayne who selected the wheel because he thought it might have the potential for bias as it was older and heavily used.

As you look at the numbers to come, please realize two things: I have not split them up into groups of 20 because they are all from the same wheel and, more importantly, I can't personally verify that no mistakes were made in recording what went down. Though I trust my three intrepid (Gary: "And underpaid!") researchers, they did spend a considerable amount of time at the wheel each day. Heidi even admits that she dozed once or twice during some stretches. ("Sorry, but this is not the most exciting thing I've ever done.")

Still, it isn't every day that you get to see the theoretical explored in reality. Not many people have actually recorded the number of spins you'll find in this book and I'm not sure any contemporary authors have recorded this many spins of *one wheel.*

Once again: Thank you to Wayne, Gary and Heidi.

Group One:

10	**22**	**24**	34	32	7	**28**
20	**17**	12	18	12	14	**4**
8	7	**2**	24	16	**8**	3
31	**24**	12	**22**	**11**	1	14
6	7	3	32	36	12	**13**
32	**8**	3	34	21	9	3
4	**31**	**28**	**31**	**29**	1	*0*
29	**20**	**28**	23	32	30	19
26	**17**	34	23	16	12	23
26	12	12	**26**	23	*00*	*0*
17	**10**	16	**22**	**8**	9	**35**
7	**33**	**4**	**31**	**20**	14	23
29	**13**	**22**	**13**	**22**	*00*	**24**
13	**4**	18	**11**	30	34	**26**
12	**6**	**28**	**29**	25	**24**	**28**
7	1	**13**	**11**	30	5	*00*
7	12	**10**	18	**10**	*0*	21
14	5	**33**	21	**2**	**29**	**8**
9	25	25	**22**	23	23	**2**
26	18	**35**	**20**	9	30	**35**
36	**33**	**2**	**35**	5	12	36
28	**29**	**26**	**29**	**29**	**20**	**20**
29	7	**31**	18	16	1	21
21	*00*	**28**	**24**	**10**	**17**	36
4	7	16	9	32	1	**35**
17	**11**	**24**	9	*00*	12	**17**
3	21	3	19	**17**	**33**	**2**
18	3	**4**	**6**	**29**	32	**28**
6	21	12	**33**	**29**	**8**	25
13	32	**35**	1	19	9	**6**
9	3	27	**17**	**26**	18	1
19	**10**	12	25	14	**31**	1
13	**35**	*00*	**13**	12	14	19
20	**22**	3	19	**29**	**11**	**13**
11	**2**	36	**24**	12	*00*	*00*
31	**35**	36	**33**	34	34	*0*
34	**28**	1	5	**29**	**13**	**17**
7	34	18	**4**	2	**2**	**8**

5	**8**	*00*	**6**	34	27	**20**
20	12	**20**	16	3	16	**11**
9	16	34	**10**	*0*	32	21
36	16	**6**	*0*	30	**35**	25
9	**2**	**10**	7	16	**4**	**26**
10	*0*	*00*	33	29	3	21
12	32	*0*	7	**35**	**31**	27
30	*00*	1	9	16	1	34
1	5	**26**	30	21	12	**8**
31	**29**	23	3	**13**	*00*	**6**
6	**10**	**15**	29	**22**	**29**	**29**
10	**8**	32	**8**	14	**26**	23
23	**20**	**26**	**10**	25	30	1
36	3	**28**	**28**	26	3	27
1	16	**6**	30	**6**	**17**	7
18	**33**	**15**	14	**13**	**31**	34
36	**31**					

Analysis of Group One Numbers: 380 Total Spins

		0. 8 hits		*00.* 12 hits		
First Dozen		1. 14	**2.** 9		3. 14	
		4. 8	5. 6		**6.** 11	
133 hits		7. 12	**8.** 11		9. 11	
		10. 12	**11.** 7		12. 18	

Second Dozen		**13.** 12	14. 8		**15.** 2	
		16. 12	**17.** 10		18. 9	
106 hits		19. 6	**20.** 11		21. 10	
		22. 8	23. 10		**24.** 8	

Third Dozen		25. 7	**26.** 12		27. 4	
		28. 11	**29.** 18		30. 9	
121 hits		**31.** 11	32. 10		**33.** 8	
		34. 12	**35.** 10		36. 9	

1st Column: 125 hits **2nd Column:** 122 hits **3rd Column:** 113 hits

Odd: 172	**Red:** 181	**High:** 174
Even: 188	**Black:** 179	**Low:** 186

Streaks:

Odd: 3 runs of 5 consecutive hits   **Even:** 3 runs of 5 consecutive hits
2 runs of 6 consecutive hits   1 run of 6 consecutive hits
1 run of 7 consecutive hits
1 run of 9 consecutive hits

Red: 4 runs of 5 consecutive hits   **Black:** 4 runs of 5 consecutive hits
1 run of 6 consecutive hits   1 run of 6 consecutive hits
1 run of 8 consecutive hits   1 run of 7 consecutive hits

High: 4 runs of 5 consecutive hits   **Low:** 2 runs of 5 consecutive hits
2 runs of 6 consecutive hits   2 runs of 6 consecutive hits
1 run of 10 consecutive hits   2 runs of 7 consecutive hits

Group Two:

21	**33**	**13**	3	5	**24**	16
18	**4**	9	3	1	12	**17**
36	*00*	36	14	4	16	25
00	**22**	3	28	1	23	12
24	19	21	**11**	**24**	**2**	**8**
00	14	12	**13**	23	1	14
25	32	**35**	24	27	16	9
23	7	12	29	**11**	**31**	21
14	25	18	20	**13**	**11**	**8**
5	**35**	*00*	**4**	25	5	**31**
24	**4**	**13**	20	**22**	**28**	36
10	5	19	25	**29**	21	*00*
24	7	**29**	35	9	**31**	*00*
9	25	**29**	**22**	32	3	**24**
34	*00*	30	23	**28**	**11**	6
14	**13**	**20**	30	**24**	9	**4**
33	**29**	23	18	19	**33**	16
27	*0*	16	18	**24**	34	**4**
7	18	**2**	3	23	9	2
3	16	**20**	**24**	36	36	**10**
1	**6**	**11**	**11**	*0*	**17**	**15**
28	1	25	**4**	**20**	19	**8**
24	16	27	**28**	**10**	**17**	3

14	3	18	19	16	21	13
5	1	27	22	9	13	29
10	12	1	25	29	35	19
24	24	1	15	22	11	33
1	00	2	13	2	36	18
4	21	2	23	8	15	31
16	16	21	32	27	19	9
35	17	12	25	29	29	14
17	23	36	10	1	00	27
20	21	30	6	0	20	0
8	2	1	8	00	27	12
6	2	30	1	36	7	1
1	26	23	15	1	9	3
31	7	28	18	5	2	18
23	18	26	24	7	1	4
3	29	11	24	31	29	33
21	9	32	19	33	31	13
24	16	3	22	25	31	2
13	27	35	27	12	00	6
34	15	31	2	27	21	28
22	7	8	23	0	32	27
33	27	19	10	0	25	2
33	8	11	34	25	10	25
23	5	21	25	27	9	5
16	3	11	8	23	13	32
11	33	19	14	11	26	34
16	27	28	36	17	1	34
36	4	3	4	12	2	29
31	36	4	25	22	18	0
20	18	6	6	33	26	9
13	3	6	9	25	20	28
19	28					

Analysis of Group Two Numbers: 380 Spins

	0.	7 hits		*00.*	11 hits	
First Dozen	**1.**	16	**2**	13	**3.**	14
	4.	12	**5.**	8	**6.**	8
127 hits	**7.**	7	**8.**	9	**9.**	12
	10.	7	**11.**	12	**12.**	9

Second Dozen	**13.** 12	14. 8	**15.** 5
	16. 14	**17.** 6	18. 12
126 hits	19. 11	**20.** 9	21. 11
	22. 9	23. 13	**24.** 16

Third Dozen	25. 16	**26.** 4	27. 14
	28. 10	**29.** 12	30. 4
109 hits	**31.** 10	32. 6	**33.** 10
	34. 6	**35.** 6	36. 11

1st Column: 130 hits **2nd Column:** 106 hits **3rd Column:** 126 hits

Odd: 195   **Red:** 202   **High:** 178
Even: 167   **Black:** 160   **Low:** 184

Streaks:

Odd: 8 runs of 5 consecutive hits **Even:** 1 run of 6 consecutive hits

Red: 5 runs of 5 consecutive hits **Black:** 3 runs of 5 consecutive hits
        1 run of 7 consecutive hits   1 run of 9 consecutive hits

High: 2 runs of 5 consecutive hits **Low:** 1 run of 7 consecutive hits
        2 runs of 6 consecutive hits   1 run of 8 consecutive hits
        1 run of 7 consecutive hits   1 run of 12 consecutive hits

Group Three:

12	1	**4**	25	**15**	*00*	**15**
00	6	**6**	19	**10**	18	**24**
14	**26**	**6**	**4**	5	*0*	36
24	3	12	*00*	**29**	3	16
18	**8**	19	*00*	**10**	12	21
8	14	**6**	**20**	34	23	21
13	16	5	**10**	**29**	**13**	**10**
23	**35**	36	**15**	21	16	14
4	**17**	25	12	9	**10**	7
15	**15**	36	3	*00*	32	3
25	9	19	**6**	1	12	**28**

9	23	25	5	23	*00*	**20**
34	**26**	32	36	9	3	36
33	19	21	**2**	**31**	32	**11**
18	**31**	**10**	21	**8**	**28**	**11**
21	9	**28**	14	14	**31**	32
00	25	12	*00*	18	25	7
12	34	27	**22**	16	**8**	36
19	**31**	12	*0*	**29**	**22**	**2**
17	**35**	**26**	**22**	1	16	7
13	9	21	9	**28**	5	**24**
31	1	25	36	*0*	32	16
8	5	23	**4**	**2**	27	**8**
27	3	**6**	*00*	23	30	23
15	**4**	**28**	**24**	**17**	**33**	9
4	**35**	16	18	25	**28**	**22**
26	34	18	14	*00*	27	25
36	32	**31**	35	3	**29**	**11**
27	32	**28**	**8**	**35**	**29**	**22**
22	**26**	**2**	5	36	*00*	**20**
00	**8**	23	36	7	**15**	**33**
33	**33**	34	18	**8**	1	34
10	**4**	30	**10**	**29**	**2**	36
9	**2**	**11**	**33**	27	12	**28**
3	**17**	14	25	25	16	**35**
31	*0*	32	5	**11**	**20**	14
19	7	**4**	**8**	25	32	**17**
10	**17**	21	34	3	**10**	21
13	7	19	**20**	19	3	19
9	36	**17**	*0*	7	9	**11**
25	25	19	**15**	**11**	**28**	21
29	**26**	16	32	**15**	**8**	**2**
35	**2**	**20**	18	**31**	**28**	27
36	27	32	**35**	**8**	**15**	**24**
2	**29**	**35**	19	16	**24**	1
8	**2**	30	**2**	**24**	**6**	**11**
17	25	*0*	**2**	*00*	**22**	23
23	**10**	**10**	18	**22**	21	**28**
3	30	**24**	**17**	**13**	16	7
2	**13**	**33**	16	3	19	**29**
20	**24**	16	3	19	23	**29**

27	9	29	19	6	12	19
14	17	34	5	18	1	11
31	32	12	17	29	17	24
36	22					

Analysis of Group Three Numbers

0. 6 hits   *00.* 13 hits

First Dozen	1.	7	**2.**	13	3.	13
	4.	8	5.	8	**6.**	8
122 hits	7.	8	**8.**	13	9.	12
	10.	12	**11.**	9	12.	11

Second Dozen	**13.**	6	14.	9	**15.**	10
	16.	13	**17.**	12	18.	10
123 hits	19.	15	**20.**	7	21.	11
	22.	9	23.	11	**24.**	10

Third Dozen	25.	15	**26.**	6	27.	9
	28.	11	**29.**	12	30.	4
116 hits	**31.**	9	32.	12	**33.**	7
	34.	8	**35.**	9	36.	14

1st Column: 121 hits **2nd Column:** 121 hits **3rd Column:** 119 hits

Odd: 183   **Red:** 190   **High:** 179
Even: 178   **Black:** 171   **Low:** 182

Streaks

Odd: 2 runs of 5 consecutive hits **Even:** 1 run of 5 consecutive hits
     1 run of 6 consecutive hits   1 run of 6 consecutive hits
     1 run of 11 consecutive hits

Red: 1 run of 5 consecutive hits **Black:** 1 run of 6 consecutive hits
     1 run of 7 consecutive hits   1 run of 7 consecutive hits

High: 2 runs of 5 consecutive hits **Low:** 2 runs of 5 consecutive hits
     1 run of 6 consecutive hits   1 run of 6 consecutive hits
     1 run of 7 consecutive hits   1 run of 7 consecutive hits
     1 run of 8 consecutive hits   1 run of 8 consecutive hits

Group Four:

35	22	6	3	29	31	12
25	9	28	3	25	12	29
10	30	32	2	1	13	11
27	19	33	0	28	10	1
12	34	34	23	7	15	33
11	19	26	12	11	31	25
6	16	28	18	13	8	7
13	35	7	8	5	14	33
0	26	25	9	7	27	00
4	12	4	30	8	10	12
9	25	17	34	31	11	35
16	34	27	00	22	16	19
22	9	33	13	33	33	5
20	27	19	31	16	32	10
22	25	8	32	31	2	15
0	8	18	10	4	26	19
22	11	20	34	0	17	0
6	27	13	7	24	21	36
13	25	13	28	15	24	28
15	36	18	24	17	25	5
3	25	30	5	11	28	34
34	23	34	23	29	35	28
33	11	5	00	1	21	18
5	3	12	32	33	16	14
31	21	12	31	16	19	28
4	2	31	16	20	15	15
35	5	6	26	4	32	31
17	0	10	28	17	28	27
12	1	1	14	16	19	15
28	16	9	18	24	2	14
0	33	6	33	28	23	33
14	32	6	7	24	23	20
19	28	23	35	7	16	11
24	31	27	2	30	8	4
33	28	14	25	19	15	17
32	6	19	24	25	7	0
17	18	25	15	18	5	00
6	3	10	23	35	11	10

21	19	25	30	**35**	**28**	12
34	**26**	5	12	**2**	**13**	3
11	**24**	**2**	**15**	26	*00*	**22**
30	23	25	19	12	**22**	32
4	**4**	**28**	5	1	**4**	32
3	**4**	**26**	27	**26**	7	**22**
27	5	*0*	**17**	12	**17**	3
11	**10**	24	36	19	34	**31**
0	**20**	35	**4**	5	21	**26**
36	**15**	*00*	7	**35**	16	1
30	*00*	9	**2**	1	21	**24**
0	30	**13**	29	**15**	36	**15**
0	25	**20**	21	14	3	**10**
21	**10**	36	**31**	*00*	**20**	**29**
17	30	*00*	**10**	**11**	12	**33**
20	**11**	1	36	**35**	**28**	5
30	36					

Analysis of Group Four Numbers: 380 Spins

0. 12 hits   *00.* 9 hits

First Dozen	1.	9	**2.**	8	3.	9
	4.	10	5.	13	**6.**	8
117 hits	7.	10	**8.**	6	9.	6
	10.	12	**11.**	13	12.	13

Second Dozen	**13.**	10	14.	7	**15.**	13
	16.	11	**17.**	10	18.	7
113 hits	19.	13	**20.**	8	21.	8
	22.	8	23.	8	**24.**	10

Third Dozen	25.	16	**26.**	9	27.	9
	28.	17	**29.**	5	30.	10
129 hits	**31.**	12	32.	9	**33.**	13
	34.	10	**35.**	11	36.	8

1st Column: 138 hits **2nd Column:** 107 hits **3rd Column:** 114 hits

Odd: 188 **Red:** 176 **High:** 184
Even: 171 **Black:** 183 **Low:** 175

Streaks:

Odd: 5 runs of 5 consecutive hits   **Even:** 2 runs of 5 consecutive hits
     1 run of 6 consecutive hits
     1 run of 7 consecutive hits

Red: 3 runs of 5 consecutive hits   **Black:** 3 runs of 5 consecutive hits
    4 runs of 6 consecutive hits

High: 2 runs of 5 consecutive hits   **Low:** 2 runs of 6 consecutive hits
    3 runs of 6 consecutive hits   1 run of 7 consecutive hits

Group Five:

10	30	**28**	**11**	**22**	21	3
27	**13**	**15**	**29**	**31**	23	16
11	**11**	**15**	23	16	**35**	**4**
8	**11**	18	19	0	**35**	3
0	30	**29**	**8**	**20**	5	**20**
3	**2**	36	25	27	**29**	**4**
3	**29**	3	**33**	**13**	32	9
9	30	**10**	9	**33**	**29**	34
3	3	**31**	3	**28**	1	**13**
00	**20**	36	**26**	**4**	**15**	**22**
16	25	16	**22**	**10**	9	**35**
14	**10**	9	**24**	**28**	1	0
19	**17**	**29**	16	3	19	25
00	**2**	25	**8**	**4**	**33**	**4**
12	27	**2**	3	**13**	**6**	36
9	7	**6**	**2**	25	23	23
6	**17**	1	14	**2**	21	25
11	23	32	25	12	**26**	1
32	**31**	1	**8**	**6**	**13**	34
3	7	**22**	**28**	**22**	**15**	19
6	27	**35**	12	**13**	0	00
28	**33**	**26**	3	3	7	1
34	**20**	19	**11**	**4**	**4**	**15**
15	**35**	**26**	14	**29**	23	**29**
15	30	34	23	**6**	**31**	12
14	7	00	**22**	**31**	00	19

18	22	19	2	12	19	24
24	2	35	1	3	12	12
5	35	11	28	12	35	22
24	21	19	2	4	14	12
26	6	29	1	28	4	17
24	4	22	24	11	15	29
14	13	1	34	10	12	30
1	10	7	15	0	29	10
18	29	35	26	33	20	14
8	7	18	2	1	34	0
4	5	26	26	34	2	11
00	9	5	36	24	24	36
34	17	3	0	26	31	27
1	34	6	7	14	14	4
7	18	5	18	26	22	33
5	5	10	18	29	35	30
19	17	31	4	2	26	00
17	7	1	36	23	36	28
13	18	35	36	15	6	24
21	5	29	32	13	2	4
11	0	14	29	2	30	35
34	27	23	00	17	3	12
23	31	11	13	26	15	32
28	19	29	18	32	20	5
20	9	21	31	20	29	15
0	00	27	13	31	10	35
20	22	0	8	4	28	18
27	1	18	00	21	18	12
7	31					

Analysis of Group Five Numbers: 380 Spins

	0. 11 hits		*00.* 10 hits	
First Dozen	1. 13	**2.** 13	3. 16	
	4. 15	5. 9	**6.** 9	
131 hits	7. 10	**8.** 6	9. 8	
	10. 9	**11.** 11	12. 12	

Second Dozen	13.	11	14.	10	15.	12
	16.	5	17.	7	18.	12
113 hits	19.	11	20.	9	21.	6
	22.	11	23.	10	24.	9

Third Dozen	25.	7	26.	12	27.	8
	28.	10	29.	17	30.	7
115 hits	31.	11	32.	6	33.	6
	34.	10	35.	13	36.	8

1st Column: 123 hits   **2nd Column:** 123 hits   **3rd Column:** 113 hits

Odd: 186   **Red:** 168   **High:** 171
Even: 173   **Black:** 191   **Low:** 188

Streaks:

Odd: 1 run of 5 consecutive hits   **Even:** 3 runs of 5 consecutive hits
       3 runs of 7 consecutive hits   1 run of 6 consecutive hits
       2 runs of 8 consecutive hits   1 run of 7 consecutive hits

Red: 1 run of 5 consecutive hits   **Black:** 3 runs of 5 consecutive hits
       1 run of 6 consecutive hits   1 run of 6 consecutive hits

High: 2 runs of 5 consecutive hits   **Low:** 3 runs of 5 consecutive hits
       1 run of 6 consecutive hits

Group Six:

8	0	19	30	7	7	8
26	14	7	4	9	22	27
0	25	31	28	24	29	17
14	35	34	0	1	33	16
20	24	21	14	25	3	32
00	16	29	1	14	21	12
29	1	19	29	32	20	13
3	2	10	1	15	5	20
7	8	30	19	11	24	33
19	33	3	29	23	13	34

27	19	9	36	35	2	31
31	29	33	32	9	11	31
32	13	31	30	19	36	35
17	11	22	20	30	0	4
21	16	28	33	13	24	11
30	28	20	36	7	1	2
00	18	12	29	13	25	31
32	17	19	1	29	15	11
34	28	19	16	5	29	00
4	4	23	0	3	18	16
27	22	28	11	4	15	33
17	20	00	12	24	16	12
3	00	20	2	8	25	2
30	8	1	24	16	1	28
24	5	4	29	15	18	12
36	6	35	36	6	29	32
13	4	18	2	9	20	5
18	9	26	27	31	20	35
0	31	35	22	24	2	36
32	29	8	14	6	8	16
5	16	18	28	21	29	5
00	11	14	33	5	32	22
19	14	36	34	0	10	26
19	3	30	32	5	19	10
4	12	11	17	10	32	29
19	7	0	11	10	1	1
11	0	26	30	27	5	31
25	00	00	19	33	28	6
11	22	27	31	15	20	34
32	20	29	18	23	23	31
4	10	19	27	22	00	16
2	11	16	15	15	18	24
33	15	1	29	15	31	31
32	13	16	23	00	11	14
21	36	16	15	9	00	22
29	4	36	16	11	9	33
28	33	19	8	1	18	7
29	7	18	21	17	35	34
36	11	6	19	36	6	16
00	35	2	24	28	20	19

20	**20**	3	**15**	**15**	**15**	**6**
00	**10**	**20**	27	12	**6**	12
11	**24**	**10**	**15**	**4**	30	**15**
18	**11**	**28**	21	**4**	9	16
12	**13**					

Analysis of Group Six Numbers: 380 Spins

	0.	9 hits	*00.*	13 hits		
First Dozen	1.	12	2.	9	3.	7
	4.	12	5.	9	**6.**	8
116 hits	7.	8	**8.**	9	9.	8
	10.	8	**11.**	17	12.	9

Second Dozen	**13.**	8	14.	8	**15.**	15
	16.	15	**17.**	6	18.	11
126 hits	19.	17	**20.**	15	21.	7
	22.	8	23.	5	**24.**	11

Third Dozen	25.	5	**26.**	**4**	27.	8
	28.	11	**29.**	18	30.	9
116 hits	**31.**	12	**32.**	**12**	**33.**	11
	34.	7	**35.**	8	36.	11

1st Column: 123 hits **2nd Column:** 120 hits **3rd Column:** 115 hits

Odd: 181	**Red:** 168	**High:** 179
Even: 177	**Black:** 190	**Low:** 179

Streaks:

Odd: 2 runs of 5 consecutive hits	**Even:** 3 runs of 5 consecutive hits
1 run of 6 consecutive hits	1 run of 7 consecutive hits
2 runs of 7 consecutive hits	

Red: no runs of 5 or more hits	**Black:** 3 runs of 5 consecutive hits
	2 runs of 6 consecutive hits
	1 run of 11 consecutive hits

High: 2 runs of 5 consecutive hits   **Low:**   2 runs of 5 consecutive hits
1 run of 6 consecutive hits   2 runs of 6 consecutive hits
2 runs of 7 consecutive hits

Group Seven:

32	25	34	17	8	23	8
15	14	2	11	27	29	3
21	00	00	3	28	32	29
20	2	35	13	10	18	13
31	23	35	28	11	22	30
34	33	8	00	15	5	22
11	19	0	8	5	7	20
26	16	5	24	17	13	12
3	29	12	26	8	27	27
18	23	23	19	25	17	20
31	19	6	00	21	26	33
15	9	19	0	7	5	28
35	21	14	35	4	9	26
19	10	15	11	9	2	13
15	14	12	17	5	36	13
23	26	2	2	14	2	1
28	16	00	30	12	6	28
12	26	30	33	28	7	1
36	35	1	9	14	36	22
28	35	21	31	19	8	25
36	4	11	31	21	11	20
29	31	20	33	12	34	30
16	24	9	19	36	29	12
12	11	15	23	27	25	00
21	29	0	27	28	21	11
3	24	21	25	15	33	10
34	2	9	32	14	10	6
10	2	19	25	2	35	34
7	8	16	19	1	11	5
25	3	31	8	14	31	23
4	31	20	5	15	34	14
15	36	7	5	34	3	32

29	**29**	**8**	**28**	**20**	*0*	**8**
34	9	**31**	21	*00*	6	**11**
29	3	**24**	8	21	**15**	21
14	7	16	19	**33**	**10**	**20**
19	**8**	21	**17**	21	**31**	19
27	34	21	**2**	**4**	**26**	*00*
8	**33**	14	23	**35**	*00*	**31**
31	19	12	**28**	1	25	**24**
22	9	**29**	8	**35**	**15**	**11**
33	9	**31**	7	**26**	**35**	**2**
31	14	**31**	24	25	**2**	**22**
10	21	23	**26**	17	**22**	27
18	**13**	3	**2**	**11**	3	*0*
21	**10**	**22**	**11**	5	**31**	12
30	**29**	25	**26**	24	12	5
7	21	14	23	**20**	9	14
35	27	**35**	**6**	**8**	*0*	34
30	**31**	30	7	5	1	1
5	**26**	23	**6**	**24**	**17**	**35**
2	12	18	18	1	30	25
16	**10**	32	36	**26**	**22**	**8**
3	25	32	**11**	**13**	*00*	**28**
24	**29**					

Analysis of Group Seven Numbers: 380 Spins

	0. 6 hits	*00.* 10 hits	
First Dozen	**1.** 8	**2.** 14	3. 10
	4. 4	5. 12	**6.** 6
124 hits	7. 9	**8.** 16	9. 10
	10. 9	**11.** 14	12 . 12
Second Dozen	**13.** 7	14. 13	**15.** 11
	16. 6	**17.** 7	18. 5
116 hits	19. 13	**20.** 9	21. 17
	22. 8	23. 11	**24.** 9
Third Dozen	25. 12	**26.** 12	27. 8
	28. 11	**29.** 12	30. 8
124 hits	**31.** 17	32. 6	**33.** 8
	34. 10	**35.** 13	36. 7

1st Column: 114 hits **2nd Column:** 139 hits **3rd Column:** 111 hits

Odd: 199   **Red:** 177   **High:** 191
Even: 165   **Black:** 187   **Low:** 173

Streaks:

Odd: 3 runs of 5 consecutive hits **Even:** 2 runs of 5 consecutive hits
       1 run of 6 consecutive hits
       1 run of 9 consecutive hits

Red: 6 runs of 5 consecutive hits **Black:** 4 runs of 5 consecutive hits
       1 run of 6 consecutive hits   2 runs of 6 consecutive hits
       1 run of 7 consecutive hits   1 run of 12 consecutive hits

High: 3 runs of 5 consecutive hits **Low:** 1 run of 5 consecutive hits
        1 run of 10 consecutive hits   3 runs of 6 consecutive hits

Group Eight:

28	34	**29**	**29**	**4**	**4**	3
16	*00*	27	5	12	27	9
35	**10**	25	30	**29**	7	**17**
23	**35**	32	**4**	24	**22**	*0*
12	16	**10**	**26**	34	**28**	25
15	16	**26**	21	24	**31**	**22**
25	**35**	9	21	19	**6**	**2**
7	19	19	12	3	**6**	**31**
15	24	**22**	**28**	32	**11**	**31**
11	26	**28**	25	**11**	14	**24**
22	2	**29**	**13**	**31**	32	7
26	1	14	*00*	**4**	5	23
00	27	16	14	19	32	**11**
5	**17**	**24**	**22**	14	**22**	27
0	**24**	**28**	25	18	27	**22**
7	32	**33**	12	**26**	21	**8**
15	20	34	**22**	32	**24**	14
25	3	**15**	**22**	14	36	36
26	**33**	**8**	**17**	1	*00*	1
14	**28**	27	**6**	18	5	**29**

31	*0*	12	**28**	25	30	**10**
00	16	30	**26**	**31**	**2**	18
29	3	25	14	21	3	27
6	**20**	19	**31**	**26**	21	**35**
9	**29**	**20**	**31**	34	**29**	**33**
14	**4**	*00*	**13**	**4**	**13**	**29**
35	25	1	34	**31**	**33**	30
10	**31**	16	36	*00*	**17**	30
1	**17**	25	34	30	**20**	16
35	23	**35**	21	**33**	5	**13**
25	**15**	36	34	21	23	21
25	**17**	*0*	**2**	**17**	7	**22**
8	7	**20**	**4**	**20**	**17**	**33**
10	3	12	**17**	27	18	34
20	**33**	**31**	14	19	**35**	**8**
6	27	25	27	**15**	**28**	*00*
9	**4**	**8**	19	36	3	25
18	1	23	**26**	**33**	**24**	**8**
24	**20**	**26**	25	*00*	21	12
20	**8**	23	36	**11**	12	**35**
28	**31**	**6**	30	1	**6**	18
32	**8**	**33**	**6**	**20**	**26**	**17**
14	**35**	36	30	18	**10**	**33**
3	**33**	**31**	7	1	**4**	**15**
19	**2**	1	**17**	1	**10**	**6**
16	5	**26**	7	30	**33**	*0*
29	36	7	**8**	32	12	**6**
24	**17**	1	7	14	**4**	**24**
28	**8**	36	**15**	27	**17**	**28**
7	25	32	1	3	14	27
26	**4**	25	**29**	18	**4**	27
3	7	19	**33**	**6**	32	7
16	**8**	18	23	12	**20**	9
31	36	5	**2**	**4**	25	**26**
13	**15**					

Analysis of Group Eight Numbers: 380 Spins

	0. 5 hits		*00.* 9 hits			
First Dozen	1.	12	**2.**	6	3.	10
	4.	13	5.	7	**6.**	11
110 hits	7.	13	**8.**	11	9.	5
	10.	7	**11.**	5	12 .	10
Second Dozen	**13.**	5	14.	13	**15.**	9
	16.	9	**17.**	13	18.	9
115 hits	19.	9	**20.**	11	21.	9
	22.	10	23.	7	**24.**	11
Third Dozen	25.	18	**26.**	14	27.	13
	28.	11	**29.**	11	30.	9
141 hits	**31.**	14	32.	10	**33.**	13
	34.	8	**35.**	10	36.	10

1st Column: 129 hits **2nd Column:** 118 hits **3rd Column:** 119 hits

Odd: 183   **Red:** 181   **High:** 198
Even: 183   **Black:** 185   **Low:** 168

Streaks:

Odd: 1 run of 5 consecutive hits **Even:** 1 run of 5 consecutive hits
  2 runs of 6 consecutive hits   3 runs of 6 consecutive hits
  1 run of 10 consecutive hits

Red: 2 runs of 5 consecutive hits **Black:** 4 runs of 5 consecutive hits
  1 run of 8 consecutive hits   1 run of 6 consecutive hits
  1 run of 9 consecutive hits   1 run of 7 consecutive hits

High: 3 runs of 5 consecutive hits **Low:** 2 runs of 5 consecutive hits
  4 runs of 6 consecutive hits   1 run of 7 consecutive hits

Group Nine:

31	20	34	11	16	33	8
12	25	00	12	25	3	6
14	1	34	16	11	35	21
10	24	7	23	5	14	20
33	34	6	0	26	4	9
27	19	32	8	31	18	36
35	30	0	34	11	16	30
29	16	10	34	3	4	1
8	22	5	0	36	10	8
34	8	29	18	29	6	23
16	27	30	4	00	6	36
16	13	32	32	5	36	24
3	1	8	23	8	16	24
25	17	35	32	32	16	26
29	3	36	22	25	30	1
27	35	9	29	34	0	9
32	23	14	28	12	7	34
22	19	25	32	25	9	17
10	9	3	14	3	7	12
26	23	24	29	00	9	36
16	11	34	17	22	4	5
24	34	30	4	11	17	19
36	00	27	12	15	21	31
21	32	10	00	8	9	14
0	26	00	16	11	1	25
31	18	32	9	15	29	3
8	8	28	13	29	17	0
11	10	12	21	10	30	16
30	34	27	7	32	12	00
29	7	0	3	20	6	9
18	11	3	18	36	27	20
16	00	26	28	0	25	12
6	36	17	22	21	29	33
29	5	26	8	6	5	00
21	36	25	19	32	12	1
16	00	22	11	31	31	25
0	15	13	21	34	12	28
6	2	24	30	34	25	15

8	23	*00*	*0*	1	**11**	**4**
30	*0*	**28**	*0*	**26**	*0*	**10**
33	9	9	*00*	24	**26**	**15**
7	5	27	32	**10**	**29**	30
14	3	**20**	23	32	14	**31**
23	16	21	25	12	32	36
20	**2**	30	27	**6**	**4**	32
7	**11**	**17**	**33**	**22**	**35**	16
17	21	9	*00*	23	**11**	**8**
28	30	9	19	18	16	*0*
29	1	**22**	**4**	36	**17**	23
4	25	**22**	**29**	**2**	**4**	9
30	32	25	9	*00*	7	**13**
4	34	7	**6**	34	**24**	32
16	1	19	**2**	**35**	36	**8**
15	**24**	5	**31**	27	**29**	**15**
19	**15**					

Analysis of Group Nine Numbers: 380 Spins

	0.	14 hits		*00.*	14 hits			
First Dozen	1.	9	**2.**	4		3.	10	
	4.	11	5.	8		**6.**	10	
122 hits	7.	9	**8.**	14		9.	15	
	10.	9	**11.**	12		12.	11	

Second Dozen	**13.**	4	14.	7		**15.**	8
	16.	17	**17.**	9		18.	6
101 hits	19.	7	**20.**	6		21.	9
	22.	9	23.	10		**24.**	9

Third Dozen	25.	14	**26.**	8		27.	9
	28.	5	**29.**	15		30.	13
129 hits	**31.**	8	32.	17		**33.**	5
	34.	16	**35.**	6		36.	13

1st Column: 118 hits   **2nd Column:** 116 hits   **3rd Column:** 118 hits

Odd: 167   **Red:** 200   **High:** 179
Even: 185   **Black:** 152   **Low:** 173

Streaks:

Odd: 1 run of 5 consecutive hits   **Even:** 1 run of 6 consecutive hits
       1 run of 6 consecutive hits   2 runs of 7 consecutive hits
       1 run of 11 consecutive hits   1 run of 12 consecutive hits

Red: 2 runs of 5 consecutive hits   **Black:** 1 run of 8 consecutive hits
       1 run of 6 consecutive hits

High: 4 runs of 5 consecutive hits   **Low:** 2 runs of 5 consecutive hits
        1 run of 6 consecutive hits   2 runs of 6 consecutive hits
        1 run of 7 consecutive hits   1 run of 8 consecutive hits

Group Ten:

10	14	18	**26**	**20**	25	**13**
13	**2**	**26**	36	**4**	**31**	36
16	**2**	5	6	8	12	**4**
12	16	19	1	**6**	**17**	**13**
14	36	**11**	12	**11**	3	*00*
31	**13**	12	**28**	7	**17**	1
31	**15**	**31**	17	*0*	**17**	8
4	**17**	19	12	25	*00*	16
7	**22**	**6**	**22**	**15**	**4**	9
1	32	**8**	**13**	19	14	12
27	7	32	1	**4**	**4**	7
29	**29**	34	**29**	**4**	**31**	1
10	32	**29**	34	**24**	32	**6**
14	**6**	27	**11**	5	25	34
3	**2**	25	1	**15**	**29**	23
14	**17**	**10**	8	**33**	*0*	**4**
31	30	21	1	7	36	21
28	34	*00*	27	14	16	**15**
16	23	**35**	**11**	**10**	**29**	18
12	32	7	9	30	23	**22**
14	**26**	16	7	21	*00*	**31**
21	19	**22**	**22**	21	32	1
21	*00*	**26**	21	16	34	**31**
36	23	7	5	**11**	**31**	7
2	18	**4**	21	**29**	21	23

15	9	34	**17**	27	*00*	27
00	**13**	**26**	12	5	**8**	**15**
8	18	**17**	**20**	**35**	5	34
33	**26**	30	**31**	23	7	*00*
24	**13**	**20**	7	**33**	**10**	36
24	1	**33**	19	21	**8**	**6**
8	27	1	**11**	25	*00*	16
4	1	**17**	**8**	**24**	**10**	21
19	23	**35**	**33**	**31**	**17**	*00*
28	16	27	**2**	36	**29**	30
21	**28**	14	**31**	27	27	19
9	**11**	*00*	**15**	21	**29**	34
28	16	21	**29**	5	36	27
1	**35**	19	36	9	**29**	**35**
27	34	36	**10**	*00*	**31**	3
16	**20**	30	32	**13**	9	**4**
7	16	9	**33**	**2**	32	**28**
10	1	**33**	32	*00*	36	**17**
1	27	**17**	*00*	**20**	19	**22**
31	**2**	**31**	12	9	**10**	**28**
12	**13**	12	**2**	3	27	*0*
5	32	**35**	12	*0*	25	14
14	**17**	19	**2**	**13**	**31**	32
13	**29**	**13**	**6**	12	**6**	**28**
31	1	7	14	**20**	**10**	21
31	**31**	36	**8**	**17**	**10**	**33**
9	**10**	**26**	12	25	9	16
26	9	25	7	**20**	3	27
19	**33**	*00*	5	**6**	**29**	21
36	**20**					

Analysis of Group Ten Numbers: 380 Spins

	0. 4 hits		*00.* 15 hits			
First Dozen	1. 16	**2.** 9		**3.** 5		
	4. 11	5. 8		**6.** 9		
125 hits	7. 14	**8.** 10		9. 11		
	10. 12	**11.** 6		12. 14		

Second Dozen	**13.**	12	14.	11	**15.**	7
	16.	13	**17.**	14	18.	4
113 hits	19.	11	**20.**	8	21.	16
	22.	6	23.	7	**24.**	4

Third Dozen	25.	8	**26.**	8	27.	14
	28.	8	**29.**	13	30.	5
123 hits	**31.**	19	32.	11	**33.**	9
	34.	9	**35.**	6	36.	13

1st Column: 139 hits   **2nd Column:** 111 hits   **3rd Column:** 111 hits

Odd: 196   **Red:** 190   **High:** 175
Even: 165   **Black:** 171   **Low:** 186

Streaks:

Odd: 4 runs of 5 consecutive hits   **Even:** 1 run of 7 consecutive hits
         1 run of 6 consecutive hits   1 run of 8 consecutive hits
         1 run of 9 consecutive hits

Red: 5 runs of 5 consecutive hits   **Black:** 2 runs of 5 consecutive hits
         1 run of 6 consecutive hits   1 run of 6 consecutive hits
                                                  1 run of 7 consecutive hits

High: 2 runs of 5 consecutive hits   **Low:** 6 runs of 5 consecutive hits
          2 runs of 6 consecutive hits   1 run of 8 consecutive hits
          1 run of 10 consecutive hits   1 run of 10 consecutive hits

Grand Totals

Number	G1	G2	G3	G4	G5	G6	G7	G8	G9	G10	Total Hits
0	8	7	6	12	11	9	6	5	14	4	**82**
00	12	11	13	9	10	13	10	9	14	15	**116**
1	14	16	7	9	13	12	8	12	9	16	**116**
2	9	13	13	8	13	9	14	6	4	9	**98**
3	14	14	13	9	16	7	10	10	10	5	**108**
4	8	12	8	10	15	12	4	13	11	11	**104**
5	6	8	8	13	9	9	12	7	8	8	**88**
6	11	8	8	8	9	8	6	11	10	9	**88**
7	12	7	8	10	10	8	9	13	9	14	**100**
8	11	9	13	6	6	9	16	11	14	10	**105**
9	11	12	12	6	8	8	10	5	15	11	**98**
10	12	7	12	12	9	8	9	7	9	12	**97**
11	7	12	9	13	11	17	14	5	12	6	**106**
12	18	9	11	13	12	9	12	10	11	14	**119**
13	12	12	6	10	11	8	7	5	4	12	**87**
14	8	8	9	7	10	8	13	13	7	11	**94**
15	2	5	10	13	12	15	11	9	8	7	**92**
16	12	14	13	11	5	15	6	9	17	13	**115**
17	10	6	12	10	7	6	7	13	9	14	**94**
18	9	12	10	7	12	11	5	9	6	4	**85**
19	6	11	15	13	11	17	13	9	7	11	**113**
20	11	9	7	8	9	15	9	11	6	8	**93**
21	10	11	11	8	6	7	17	9	9	16	**104**
22	8	9	9	8	11	8	8	10	9	6	**86**
23	10	13	11	8	10	5	11	7	10	7	**92**
24	8	16	10	10	9	11	9	11	9	4	**97**
25	7	16	15	16	7	5	12	18	14	8	**118**
26	12	4	6	9	12	4	12	14	8	8	**89**
27	4	14	9	9	8	8	8	13	9	14	**96**
28	11	10	11	17	10	11	11	11	5	8	**105**
29	18	12	12	5	17	18	12	11	15	13	**133**
30	9	4	4	10	7	9	8	9	13	5	**78**
31	11	10	9	12	11	12	17	14	8	19	**123**
32	10	6	12	9	6	12	6	10	17	11	**99**
33	8	10	7	13	6	11	8	13	5	9	**90**
34	12	6	8	10	10	7	10	8	16	9	**96**
35	10	6	9	11	13	8	13	10	6	6	**92**
36	9	11	14	8	8	11	7	10	13	13	**104**

Total Odd: 1,850   Total Red: 1,833   Total High: 1,808
Total Even: 1,752   Total Black: 1,769   Total Low: 1,794

Total 1st Dozen: 1,227   Total 2nd Dozen: 1,152   Total 3rd Dozen: 1,223

Total 1st Column: 1,260   Total 2nd Column: 1,183   Total 3rd Column: 1,159

Streaks Total:

Odd: 30 runs of 5 consecutive hits **Even:** 15 runs of 5 consecutive hits
10 runs of 6 consecutive hits   8 runs of 6 consecutive hits
6 runs of 7 consecutive hits   6 runs of 7 consecutive hits
2 runs of 8 consecutive hits   1 run of 8 consecutive hits
2 runs of 9 consecutive hits   1 run of 9 consecutive hits
2 runs of 11 consecutive hits   1 run of 12 consecutive hits

Red: 29 runs of 5 consecutive hits **Black:** 26 runs of 5 consecutive hits
9 runs of 6 consecutive hits   9 runs of 6 consecutive hits
3 runs of 7 consecutive hits   4 runs of 7 consecutive hits
2 runs of 8 consecutive hits   1 run of 8 consecutive hits
1 run of 9 consecutive hits   1 run of 9 consecutive hits
                                       1 run of 11 consecutive hits
                                       1 run of 12 consecutive hits

High: 26 runs of 5 consecutive hits **Low:** 20 runs of 5 consecutive hits
17 runs of 6 consecutive hits   12 runs of 6 consecutive hits
5 runs of 7 consecutive hits   6 runs of 7 consecutive hits
1 run of 8 consecutive hits   4 runs of 8 consecutive hits
3 runs of 10 consecutive hits   1 run of 10 consecutive hits
                                       1 run of 12 consecutive hits

Number	Hits	Frequency	Bias Rating
29	133	1 in 28.56	B
31	123	1 in 30.89	PB
12	119	1 in 31.93	MB
25	118	1 in 32.20	MB
00	116	1 in 32.75	MB/R
1	116	1 in 32.75	MB/R

Comments

I think there is a strong possibility that the wheel we've just tracked shows evidence of one and, perhaps, two distinctly biased numbers: number **29** with 133 hits and number **31** with 123 hits. However, I think you could make a strong case that a whole section of this wheel shows a bias. If you look at the numbers that hit with relatively great frequency, you'll note that 1, *00*, 12, 25, **29,** and **31** are all contained within a section of 10 numbers that also includes: number 27 with 96 hits (four under the theoretical average of 100 hits); number **10** with 97 hits (three under the theoretical average); **8** with 105 hits (five over the theoretical average); 19 with 113 hits (13 over the theoretical average). Another interesting fact is that this ten-number slice is fenced in by two numbers that have hit at a relatively low frequency — on the one end by number **13** that hit just 87 times and on the other end by number 18 that hit just 85 times. Since a ten-number slice should hit an average of 1,000 times in 3,800 spins, the fact that our ten-section slice (which includes two numbers that were below average) hit 1,136 times would indicate that it is indeed potentially worth betting.

12

A Final Word
and Recommended Reading

There are some excellent roulette books on the market. There are also many excellent roulette sections in books about gambling games in general. The problem with all the books that I am recommending is — strangely enough — the truth. The truth about roulette is not pleasant. Unless you are attacking the actual mechanism itself through biased-wheel play (Big Number and/or sector slicing) or visual/computer tracking, you're going to lose in the long run. That's the awful truth. Unpleasantly enough, the long run in roulette, especially on the double-zero American wheel, is a lot shorter than the long run for many other casino games owing to the enormous 5.26 percent house edge. With such an edge, you will find that while the game will fluctuate up and down, down and up, between you and the casino, the downs will occur with greater frequency than the ups. The bigger the house edge, the faster the player gets nailed. Even the single-zero European wheel is no bargain at 2.70 percent. Perhaps the only roulette game worth considering for the layout player is the one with the *en prison* rule on the even-money bets that reduces the vig to 1.35 percent. No matter how upbeat or positive one's attitude is when writing about such a game, there really is no way to gloss over this fact: roulette *on an unbiased wheel* is a bankroll killer.

To see clearly where roulette stacks up against various other casino games, consider that the card counter in blackjack plays with an edge over the casino (albeit a small one); that the Captain's methods at craps can reduce the house edge to zero and in some cases, as in buying bets from other players, actually give the player a small edge; that baccarat and mini-baccarat, two excellent but usually overlooked games, carry smallish edges hovering towards the one percent range; and that even such house-friendly games as Let it Ride and Three Card Poker have lower overall edges than does roulette on an unbiased double-zero wheel. It is no secret that your money will not last long if roulette is your game of choice.

If you are going to play roulette you have to be tremendously disciplined and not a little skittish. Give yourself a certain amount to play with (depending on the strategy selected) and if you lose that amount, call it a night. Conversely, if Lady Luck is smiling on you, then take some of your winnings and put them aside to guarantee that you go home a winner. Roulette stripped many a nobleman of his wealth and good name; don't let it do that to you. Play smart and play scared.

The following books contain interesting information concerning strategies and/or the history of the game. While I don't necessarily endorse all the strategies given by all of the authors, all of them are worth reading and adding to your gaming bookshelf. Many of the books (or booklets) I'm recommending can't be found in mainstream bookshops but must be ordered from the publisher directly or from a bookstore that specializes in gaming books.

The Julian Strategies in Roulette by John F. Julian. Paone Press, Box 610, Lynbrook, NY 11563 or 1-800-944-0406. ($16.95)
This is a clear, intelligent analysis of the game and the many approaches for beating it. Fully develops a method for clocking wheels and clocking players, as well as Big Number play and sector slicing. Has some fun layout strategies.

Beating the Wheel by Russell T. Barnhart. Carol Publishing Company, 600 Madison Avenue, New York, NY 10022. ($12.95)

Want to read all about the great adventures of the great biased-wheel players of all time? Then this is the book for you. Fully half of the book dwells on the exciting exploits of these wheel-tracking pioneers. The other half of the book is an exhaustive, interesting and compelling analysis of how to tackle biased wheels and Big Numbers. It's a little heavy on the math but accessible to the general reader nevertheless. May be out of print as I write this which is a shame. Barnhart has played roulette all over the world and this book is filled with flavor.

The Eudaemonic Pie by Thomas A. Bass. Vintage Books, 201 E. 50th St., New York, NY 10022. ($5.95)

This book chronicles the often hilarious, often serious, but never dull adventures of a group of computer wizards as they try to beat the wheel by using a hidden computer in their shoes. They aren't fully successful, although they prove that it can be done, but it's a great story and a good read. You won't learn any strategies from Mr. Bass but if you like reading about the human adventure in gambling, this book is the one for you. Bass has an engaging style.

The Biased-Wheel Handbook by Mark Billings and Brent Fredrickson. Saros Designs Publishing. Order through RGE Publishing, 414 Santa Clara Ave., Oakland, CA 94610 ($79.95)

This spiral-bound book, with software, is for serious players who really want to dig into the statistical information and analyses necessary to find evidence of wheel biases — however subtle such evidence might be. While the book is heavy on the math, the authors have intelligently divided each chapter into two parts: the first part deals with their ideas and findings in a way that a non-mathematician can easily understand; the second part displays the math or logic involved in a more detailed way for those who enjoy their math straight up without a chaser. You would think that a book so heavy on the numbers would lack personality. Not so. The two authors have a fun, irreverent style that makes the book a surprisingly good read. They also speak with authority. You might want to use the software in this book to analyze on your own the 3,800 spins that I have recorded on one wheel in Chapter Eleven. The price tag is heavy and the book is not usually found even in gambling bookstores but has to be ordered through RGE Publishing. However, if you want to become a consummate wheel tracker, this is the book that might do it for you.

How to Beat Roulette by Laurance Scott. PO Box V, Dona Ana, NM 88032. (Complete system: $295.00)

This is another high-priced but valuable three-part learning program that features a book and a video. Again it is only for roulette players who are dedicated and want to become semiprofessional or professional players. Scott lays out everything you need to know to become a visual wheel tracker and he estimates that with this system you will play with a 25 to 40 percent edge over the house. According to those who have seen Scott in action, he is the real thing. His system is not easy to learn and for those of you who get nauseous watching a roulette wheel spin and spin, you might have to give up before you throw up. I gave up. Still, if you have the stomach and the endurance for it, visual wheel tracking could be the way to the vault.

How to Win at Roulette by Norman Squire. Oldcastle Books, 18 Coleswood Rd., Harpenden, Herts, AL5 1EQ, England. Approximately $10.00.

First published in 1968 and now republished by Oldcastle Books, this is *the* book for those roulette players who want to play the layout. While none of the hundreds of strategies explored can turn the game in your favor, you will enjoy the discussions and lessons of Mr. Squire. You will also note the deadly earnestness of the European roulette aficionado as Squire delves into the layout strategies the way a philosopher delves into questions of being and nothingness. The book lays out all the common layout strategies and a multitude of variations plainly and then gives you practice exercises so that you can become proficient at the techniques. It's an interesting read even though it tells you more about the psychology of the serious roulette player than it does how to actually beat the game.

The Mathematics of Gambling by Edward O. Thorp. Gambling Times Books, 16760 Stagg St. #213, Van Nuys, CA 91406. ($7.95)

Dr. Thorp is the father of card counting in blackjack and a mathematics whiz to boot. His discussion of roulette and his attempts to beat it by building a roulette computer to defeat the casinos is fascinating. While the book also concerns forms of gambling other than roulette, the section on roulette is worth the price of the book. It is amazing how many great minds — from Pascal to Thorp — have flirted with that spinning wheel.

Gambling Scams by Darwin Ortiz. Lyle Stuart, Inc., Carol Publishing Group, 600 Madison Ave., New York, NY 10022. ($10.95)

This is a wonderful book about all forms of casino cheating — both by the players and by the casinos. Although its main focus is not roulette, the book still gives valuable insights into how gambling sharks go about making the rest of us their bloody chum. This book might help you stay out of dangerous waters. Worth reading as a cautionary exercise. Darwin Ortiz goes into great detail concerning all forms of cheating. Once you've read this book you'll never look at any game in quite the same way again.

The Only Game in Town: A Illustrated History of Gambling by Hank Messick and Burt Goldblatt. Thomas Y. Crowell Company, New York, NY 10019. ($12.95)

This is a coffee-table book from the 1970s but it is well worth searching for. Gives you the history behind many of today's games and the photographs are invaluable. It's like stepping into a time machine. It is always interesting to note that the games one plays today are essentially the games that people have always played, in one variation or another. I guess the more things change, the more they remain the same.

The Complete Illustrated Guide to Gambling by Alan Wyckes. Doubleday and Company, New York, NY 10036. ($9.95)

This is another book that you might have trouble finding but it is the best source of historical information concerning all forms of gambling that I've ever read. I love this book and I refer to it constantly. Has wonderful photographs and great insights into gambling and people. It is a riveting read. Search for it. Great roulette information, too. Wyckes is a writer with full command of the language and knowledge of gaming. He's a great stylist and the book has nary a dull moment.

Reference Guide to Casino Gambling by Henry J. Tamburin. Research Services Unlimited, Box 19727, Greensboro, NC 27419. ($15.00)

Good general book on casino games with a strong section on roulette. Henry Tamburin is a gaming writer whose writing is clear and his advice sound. Tamburin gives good money-management advice for anyone interested in tackling the wheel.

Beat the Casino by Frank Barstow. Pocket Books, 1230 Avenue of the Americas, New York, NY 10020. ($4.50)

I don't even know if this book is still in print but I do know that Barstow is one fun read. If you like systems, Barstow gives them to you aplenty. As for layout strategies in roulette, Barstow has quite a few. While I don't necessarily recommend playing many of the systems he suggests, I do enjoy the way he suggests them. Have fun.

Smart Casino Gambling by Olaf Vancura. Index Publishing Group, Inc., 3368 Governor Drive, Suite 273, San Diego, CA 92122. ($24.95)

This is a book that covers many casino games and has a good section on roulette. Vancura is a mathematician who clearly explains the principles behind probability in a pleasing and relatively easy-to-understand way. He has some interesting anecdotal stories as well.

The Winner's Guide to Casino Gambling by Edwin Silberstang. Plume Books, 111 Fifth Ave., New York, NY 10003. ($9.95)

Another good general casino book with a particularly interesting section on roulette. Silberstang is a good stylist and his anecdotes and stories are well-written, enlightening and fun to read.

Action Play Roulette Tracker Card developed by Joe Zanghi. Action Play, P.O. Box 2424, Cherry Hill, NJ 08002. ($6.95 for card only; $24.95 for card and index keys)

If you want to record short-term hits of numbers to see if there are potential biases in the wheel, this device is the way to go. You can order either the American double-zero card or the European single-zero card. The index keys are helpful for making quick decisions on which sections and numbers to bet. Comes with a guide and erasable marker pen for recording numbers.

Newsletters and Magazines

There are no newsletters or magazines at this time devoted solely to roulette. Most newsletters are for blackjack aficionados and there are one or two for craps lovers. However, my own newsletter, *Chance and Circumstance,* Paone Press, Box 610, Lynbrook, NY 11563 or 1-800-944-0406 ($40 per year), will often contain articles on roulette. Many of the insights contained in this book first appeared in *Chance and Circumstance.*

Glossary

A cheval: French for the split bet.

Action: The amount of money you wager over a given period of time. Used as a basis of judgment for comps.

Action player: A player who bets big and for long periods of time. Sometimes used as a euphemism for stupid player.

Adrenotrend system: See *hot and cold system.*

American wheel: Roulette wheel that has *0* and *00* pockets.

Backtrack: The outer, stationary rim of the roulette wheel where the ball is spun.

Bankroll: The total amount of money a gambler sets aside to gamble with.

Biased wheel: A roulette wheel that has an imperfection which shows up by certain numbers or sections appearing out of all proportion to their probability.

Biased wheel play: Ascertaining and then betting according to the bias of a wheel.

Big Number: A number that has hit more than its theoretical average.

Black action: A bet made with a black ($100) chip.

Black bet: A wager that the next number will be black.

Blacks: Chips valued at $100.

Bottom track: The slanting, stationary, inner area of a roulette wheel down which the ball slides into the pockets.

Cancellation betting system: A betting system using a series of numbers that cancels numbers after winning a bet and adds numbers after losing a bet. Also known as the *Labouchere System.*

Capping a bet: Adding more chips to a bet that has already won. Also known as *past posting.*

Carre: French term for the corner bet.

Casino advantage: The edge, usually shown as a percentage, that the house has over the player.

Casino host: The person responsible for seeing that high rollers are treated with the dignity and graciousness their wallets merit.

Casino manager: The person responsible for seeing that the games of a given casino are handled properly.

Chameleon Strategy: Looking for players who have been winning and then mimicking their betting patterns in the hope that they will continue to be lucky, have found biased wheels, or are visual wheel trackers.

Chasing losses: Increasing your bets in order to recoup what you've lost. Not a good way to play.

Check rack: The tray that holds the chips for a game. Also known as *chip rack* or *chip tray.*

Checks: Another name for chips.

Choppy game: A game where neither the player nor the house has been winning consistently. Or, a game where no discernible streaks or patterns have been appearing.

Clocking: Keeping track of the results of roulette spins to ascertain whether a wheel is biased.

Clocking players: Watching to see which players have been winning in order to mimic their betting patterns.

Color up: To exchange smaller denomination chips for larger denomination chips at a table.

Cold table: Any table where you and/or other players have been losing.

Colonne: The French term for column bet.

Column bet: A bet on one of the columns of numbers.

Combination bet: A bet with one chip on two or more numbers.

Comp: The "freebies" that casinos give out for certain levels of betting.

Corner bet: A bet that four numbers in a given segment of the layout will win. Also known as a *square bet* or a *quarter bet.*

Credit line: The amount of credit a player is allowed by a given casino.

Credit manager: The person in charge of determining casino credit for the players.

Crew: Personnel who man a game.

Crossroader: A casino cheat.

Croupier: French term for dealer in roulette.

d'Alembert betting system: A system of betting where you increase your bet by one unit after a loss and decrease your bet by one unit after a win.

Dead table: A table that is manned and ready for action but has no players.

Dealer: The casino employee who staffs the games offered.

Derniere: A French term for last as in columns or dozens bets.

Double-Up system of betting: Also known as the *Martingale System.* A player doubles his bet after each loss hoping to recoup all his previous losses and win the initial bet.

Double-zero wheel: Another name for the American roulette wheel that has *0* and *00.*

Douzaine: A French term for the dozen bet.

Dozen bet: A bet that one of 12 numbers in sequence will appear.

Double dynamite roulette system: A combination of Big Number play and sector slicing for short-range play.

Drop: The casino term for the total amount of money and markers wagered at the tables.

Drop box: Where the money is dropped after the player cashes into a game and receives his chips. The box is usually located under the table.

Dumping: A casino table that is losing money to the players.

Edge: Having the advantage in a game.

En plein: The French term for the straight up bet.

En prison: French term for the favorable option found in single-zero roulette. Player doesn't lose his even-money bets if the zero shows. Instead the bet is locked up for another spin. If the bet wins, it is returned fully. If the bet loses, the house collects it.

European wheel: Also known as the single-zero wheel. Has one 0.

Even bet: A wager that one of the even numbers will win the next spin.

Even money: A bet that pays off at one to one.

Even up: A bet that has no mathematical edge for either side.

Eye in the sky: The cameras, usually in bubbles, located throughout the casino that videotape the action.

Fair game: A game where neither the house nor the player has the edge.

Fibonacci betting system: The progressive betting system where each bet is a combination of the two previous numbers. (i.e., 1, 2, 3, 5, 8, 13, etc.)

Five-number bet: Can only be made on the American wheel. Single wager that 0, 00, 1, **2,** or 3 will hit next. The single worst bet in roulette.

Flat bettor: A player who never varies the size of his bets but bets the same amount each time.

Floorman: Individual responsible for supervising several tables in the pit.

Fluctuation in probability: Numbers randomly appearing out of all proportion to their probability. A short sequence of repeating decisions. A mathematical term that means good or bad luck depending on whether the fluctuation is in your favor or not.

French wheel: Same as *European wheel.*

Front money: Money previously deposited in the cage and used by the player to draw markers against.

Gaffed wheel: A wheel that has been rigged.

Gambling stake: Amount of money reserved for gambling. Same thing as a *bankroll.*

George: A good tipper.

Gland Martingale: Tongue in cheek name for a limited Martingale of two steps after a predetermined number of even-money decisions has occurred.

Golden numbers: Numbers that have hit out of all proportion to their probability. Might be an indication that a wheel is biased.

Grand Martingale: A betting system where you double your bets and add one extra unit after a loss.

Greens: Chips valued at $25.

Grifter: A scam artist.

Grind: A small money player.

Grind down: The casino winning all of a player's money due to the advantage it has on bets.

Grind joint: A casino that caters to *low rollers* or small-money players.

Grind system: Increasing one's bet a unit after each win. Any system that attempts to win small amounts frequently against the casinos.

Guerrilla gambling: The combination of smart play and hit-and-run tactics to beat the casinos at their own games.

Heat: Intensive scrutiny of a player's action to determine if he has an edge either due to cheating or to expertise.

High: The numbers 19-36.

High roller: A person who plays for big money.

Hoca: Early version of roulette.

Hot and cold system: A wager on the side that won previously. Another name for the streak method of betting.

Hot table: A table where the players have been winning.

House edge: The mathematical edge that the casino has on a given bet.

House odds: The payoff that reflects the casino's tax on your winning bet.

House person: A dealer who is unusually concerned with the casino's profits. A dealer who identifies with the casino or enjoys watching players lose.

Hustler: A gambling cheat.

Inside bet: A bet made on the central, numbered portion of the roulette layout.

Impair: The French term for the *odd bet.*

Labouchere betting system: See *cancellation betting system.*

Layout: The design imprinted with the various bets.

Layout strategies: Betting systems and strategies that try to overcome the house edge without trying to determine if the wheel is biased.

Line bet: A single bet that one of six numbers will win.

Long end of the bet: The side of the bet that must pay off more than it collects.

Long run: The concept that a player could play so often that probability would tend to even out. That is, you would start to see the total appearance of numbers or colors, etc., and approximate what probability theory predicts. A long-run player is one who plays a lot!

Low: The numbers 1-18.

Low roller: A person who bets small stakes.

Manque: The French term for *low* in roulette.

Mark: An individual who has been or is going to be cheated. A sucker.

Marker: The check that a player fills out before receiving casino credit at the table. A promissory note of IOU.

Martingale system of wagering: Doubling your bet after a loss.

Match play: A casino promotion where players are given special chips that they can bet. They are paid off in regular casino chips on a win.

Money at risk: Money that has been wagered and can be lost.

Money management: The methods a player uses to save his bankroll from ruin.

Money plays: The call that alerts the dealer and the pit that you are betting cash and not chips.

Mucker: Anyone who uses sleight-of-hand techniques to cheat.

Negative progression: Any system of wagering where you increase bets after a loss.

Nickel: A five dollar chip that is usually red.

No action: A call made by a dealer that the casino will not cover a particular bet. Or that a particular spin or decision doesn't count.

Noir: The French term for black.

Odd bet: A bet that the next number will be odd.

Odds: The likelihood of an event happening.

On the square: A game that is honest.

Outside bets: One of the 2-to-1 or even-money bets found on the outside of the roulette layout.

Paddle: The tool used to push the money into the drop box.

Pair: The French term for even.

Parlay: To double one's bet after a win.

Passe: The French term for *high* in roulette. The numbers 19-36.

Past posting: Placing a winning wager *after* a decision has been reached. Usually done by *capping a bet.*

Patience system: A grind method of playing whereby the player waits for a certain number of decisions before placing a bet.

P.C.: The house edge expressed as a percentage.

Penny ante: A game played for small stakes.

Pinching: Illegally removing chips from a bet after an unfavorable decision.

Pit: An area consisting of a number of gaming tables.

Pit boss: The individual in charge of a pit.

Power of the pen: The ability to issue hotel comps to players on the part of some casino executives.

Premiere: The French term for first.

Premium players: A casino term meaning big bettors or players with big credit lines.

Press: To increase the amount wagered, usually by doubling it, after a win.

Push: A tie.

Quarter bet: A wager that one of four numbers will be hit on the next spin. Same as *corner bet* and *square bet.*

Quarters: Chips valued at $25. Usually green.

Rating: Evaluating the player's action for the purposes of comps.

Rating card: The card used for rating a player.

Red bet: An even-money bet that the next decision will be red.

Reds: Casino chips worth five dollars.

RFB: Complimentary room, food and beverage.

Rouge: The French term for red.

Ruin or element of ruin: Losing your bankroll. The probability of losing every penny of your bankroll.

Scam: Any scheme to defraud a player or casino.

Scared money: Money a player can't afford to lose.

Scobe's wager: If it doesn't hurt to play as if something is true then you have nothing to lose by playing this way as long as you don't increase your time or risk at a table.

Section (sector) shooter: A dealer who tries to hit certain numbers or sections on the wheel.

Section shooting: The act of placing the ball in a given section of the wheel.

Section slicing: Dividing a wheel into sections based upon which numbers have been hitting for the purpose of discovering biases.

Session: A given period of play at a casino game. Usually terminated at a predetermined time, or at a certain level of wins or losses.

Session stake: The amount of money set aside for one session of play.

Shift boss: The individual in charge of the casino during a given work shift.

Shill: An individual employed by the casino to play games that are being underplayed.

Short end: The side of the bet that has to pay off less than it will win.

Short odds: Less than the true odds payoff for a bet.

Short run: The limited amount of time during any given session when probability theory will seemingly be skewered by streaks or fluctuations.

Signature: The unconscious ability of a dealer to place a ball within a given distance from the last hit.

Single-zero wheel: The *European wheel* that has only one *0*.

Sixain: The French term for the *six number bet*.

Six number bet: A single bet that one of six numbers will hit on the next spin.

Split bet: A single bet that one of two particular numbers will hit on the next spin.

Spread: The difference between the minimum and maximum bets a player makes.

Square bet: A bet that one of four particular numbers will hit on the next spin. See *quarter bet* and *corner bet*.

Squares: A game that is on the level or honest; or a player who is on the level or honest.

Stack: A group of 20 roulette chips.

Straight up bet: An inside bet on one number.

Street bet: A bet that one of three particular numbers will hit on the next spin.

Surrender: The option whereby a casino only takes half a player's losing wager on the even-money bets when the *0* or *00* hits.

Sweat: Casinos who are upset by players winning or having

skill are said to "sweat" out their games. Also, a player who is losing and is worried.

Table hopping: Moving from table to table in a casino.

Take down: To recall a wager before a decision.

Tapped out: To lose one's entire bankroll.

Toke: Another word for tip.

Toke hustler: A dealer who tries to get players to tip him.

Tom: A poor tipper.

Tough out: The Captain's term for a player who doesn't beat himself.

Transversale: The French term for the triple or trio bet. Three number bet.

Trio bet: A single bet that the next spin will result in one of three numbers.

True odds: The actual probability of an event happening.

Underground joint: An illegal casino.

Vic: Sucker. Short for victim.

Vig or vigorish: The casino tax on a bet. Also known as *juice*.

Visual wheel tracking: The ability to judge where the ball will land by sight.

Wager: Another term for bet.

Wheel: Short for roulette wheel.

Wheel strategies: Strategies that try to exploit imperfections in the wheel in order for the player to get the edge.

Wheel chips: Special chips used only for roulette.

Wheel head: The portion of the roulette wheel that contains the numbered pockets.

Wheel roller: A roulette dealer.

Index